RICHARD NIXON

RICHARD NIXON

C. Peter Ripley

CHELSEA HOUSE PUBLISHERS
NEW YORK
NEW HAVEN   PHILADELPHIA

EDITOR-IN-CHIEF: Nancy Toff
EXECUTIVE EDITOR: Remmel T. Nunn
MANAGING EDITOR: Karyn Gullen Browne
COPY CHIEF: Juliann Barbato
ART DIRECTOR: Giannella Garrett
MANUFACTURING MANAGER: Gerald Levine

Staff for RICHARD NIXON:

SENIOR EDITOR: John W. Selfridge
ASSISTANT EDITORS: Maria Behan, Pierre Hauser, Kathleen McDermott,
                  Bert Yaeger
EDITORIAL ASSISTANT: James Matthew Guiry
COPY EDITORS: Gillian Bucky, Sean Dolan, Ellen Scordato
PICTURE EDITOR: Juliette Dickstein
DESIGN ASSISTANT: Jill Goldreyer
PICTURE RESEARCH: Juliette Dickstein, Matthew Miller
LAYOUT: David Murray
PRODUCTION COORDINATOR: Laura McCormick
COVER ILLUSTRATION: © Michael Garland

CREATIVE DIRECTOR: Harold Steinberg

Frontispiece courtesy of The Library of Congress

3 5 7 9 8 6 4 2

Library of Congress Cataloging in Publication Data

Ripley, C. Peter. RICHARD NIXON

(World leaders past & present)
Bibliography: p. 108
Includes index.
1. Nixon, Richard M. (Richard Milhous), 1913–
—Juvenile literature. 2. Presidents—United States—
Biography—Juvenile literature. 3. United States—Politics
and government—1969–1974—Juvenile literature.
[1. Nixon, Richard M. (Richard Milhous), 1913–
2. Presidents. 3. United States—Politics and government—
1969–1974]
I. Title. II. Series: World leaders past & present.
E856.R57   1987   973.924′092′4 [B] [92]
87-10278

ISBN 0-87754-585-5

Contents

"On Leadership," Arthur M. Schlesinger, jr. 7

1. The Early Years... 13
2. The Road to Success... 25
3. Grand Ambitions, Great Disappointments 37
4. "The New Nixon" 55
5. The Nixon Presidency: Foreign Affairs 75
6. Policy at Home 91
7. The Politician 103
Further Reading... 108
Chronology.. 109
Index... 110

ADENAUER
ALEXANDER THE GREAT
MARC ANTONY
KING ARTHUR
ATATÜRK
ATTLEE
BEGIN
BEN-GURION
BISMARCK
LÉON BLUM
BOLÍVAR
CESARE BORGIA
BRANDT
BREZHNEV
CAESAR
CALVIN
CASTRO
CATHERINE THE GREAT
CHARLEMAGNE
CHIANG KAI-SHEK
CHURCHILL
CLEMENCEAU
CLEOPATRA
CORTÉS
CROMWELL
DANTON
DE GAULLE
DE VALERA
DISRAELI
EISENHOWER
ELEANOR OF AQUITAINE
QUEEN ELIZABETH I
FERDINAND AND ISABELLA
FRANCO

FREDERICK THE GREAT
INDIRA GANDHI
MOHANDAS GANDHI
GARIBALDI
GENGHIS KHAN
GLADSTONE
GORBACHEV
HAMMARSKJÖLD
HENRY VIII
HENRY OF NAVARRE
HINDENBURG
HITLER
HO CHI MINH
HUSSEIN
IVAN THE TERRIBLE
ANDREW JACKSON
JEFFERSON
JOAN OF ARC
POPE JOHN XXIII
LYNDON JOHNSON
JUÁREZ
JOHN F. KENNEDY
KENYATTA
KHOMEINI
KHRUSHCHEV
MARTIN LUTHER KING, JR.
KISSINGER
LENIN
LINCOLN
LLOYD GEORGE
LOUIS XIV
LUTHER
JUDAS MACCABEUS
MAO ZEDONG

MARY, QUEEN OF SCOTS
GOLDA MEIR
METTERNICH
MUSSOLINI
NAPOLEON
NASSER
NEHRU
NERO
NICHOLAS II
NIXON
NKRUMAH
PERICLES
PERÓN
QADDAFI
ROBESPIERRE
ELEANOR ROOSEVELT
FRANKLIN D. ROOSEVELT
THEODORE ROOSEVELT
SADAT
STALIN
SUN YAT-SEN
TAMERLANE
THATCHER
TITO
TROTSKY
TRUDEAU
TRUMAN
VICTORIA
WASHINGTON
WEIZMANN
WOODROW WILSON
XERXES
ZHOU ENLAI

ON LEADERSHIP
Arthur M. Schlesinger, jr.

LEADERSHIP, it may be said, is really what makes the world go round. Love no doubt smooths the passage; but love is a private transaction between consenting adults. Leadership is a public transaction with history. The idea of leadership affirms the capacity of individuals to move, inspire, and mobilize masses of people so that they act together in pursuit of an end. Sometimes leadership serves good purposes, sometimes bad; but whether the end is benign or evil, great leaders are those men and women who leave their personal stamp on history.

Now, the very concept of leadership implies the proposition that individuals can make a difference. This proposition has never been universally accepted. From classical times to the present day, eminent thinkers have regarded individuals as no more than the agents and pawns of larger forces, whether the gods and goddesses of the ancient world or, in the modern era, race, class, nation, the dialectic, the will of the people, the spirit of the times, history itself. Against such forces, the individual dwindles into insignificance.

So contends the thesis of historical determinism. Tolstoy's great novel *War and Peace* offers a famous statement of the case. Why, Tolstoy asked, did millions of men in the Napoleonic wars, denying their human feelings and their common sense, move back and forth across Europe slaughtering their fellows? "The war," Tolstoy answered, "was bound to happen simply because it was bound to happen." All prior history predetermined it. As for leaders, they, Tolstoy said, "are but the labels that serve to give a name to an end and, like labels, they have the least possible connection with the event." The greater the leader, "the more conspicuous the inevitability and the predestination of every act he commits." The leader, said Tolstoy, is "the slave of history."

Determinism takes many forms. Marxism is the determinism of class. Nazism the determinism of race. But the idea of men and women as the slaves of history runs athwart the deepest human instincts. Rigid determinism abolishes the idea of human freedom—

the assumption of free choice that underlies every move we make, every word we speak, every thought we think. It abolishes the idea of human responsibility, since it is manifestly unfair to reward or punish people for actions that are by definition beyond their control. No one can live consistently by any deterministic creed. The Marxist states prove this themselves by their extreme susceptibility to the cult of leadership.

More than that, history refutes the idea that individuals make no difference. In December 1931 a British politician crossing Park Avenue in New York City between 76th and 77th Streets around 10:30 P.M. looked in the wrong direction and was knocked down by an automobile—a moment, he later recalled, of a man aghast, a world aglare: "I do not understand why I was not broken like an eggshell or squashed like a gooseberry." Fourteen months later an American politician, sitting in an open car in Miami, Florida, was fired on by an assassin; the man beside him was hit. Those who believe that individuals make no difference to history might well ponder whether the next two decades would have been the same had Mario Constasino's car killed Winston Churchill in 1931 and Giuseppe Zangara's bullet killed Franklin Roosevelt in 1933. Suppose, in addition, that Adolf Hitler had been killed in the street fighting during the Munich *Putsch* of 1923 and that Lenin had died of typhus during World War I. What would the 20th century be like now?

For better or for worse, individuals do make a difference. "The notion that a people can run itself and its affairs anonymously," wrote the philosopher William James, "is now well known to be the silliest of absurdities. Mankind does nothing save through initiatives on the part of inventors, great or small, and imitation by the rest of us—these are the sole factors in human progress. Individuals of genius show the way, and set the patterns, which common people then adopt and follow."

Leadership, James suggests, means leadership in thought as well as in action. In the long run, leaders in thought may well make the greater difference to the world. But, as Woodrow Wilson once said, "Those only are leaders of men, in the general eye, who lead in action. . . . It is at their hands that new thought gets its translation into the crude language of deeds." Leaders in thought often invent in solitude and obscurity, leaving to later generations the tasks of imitation. Leaders in action—the leaders portrayed in this series—have to be effective in their own time.

And they cannot be effective by themselves. They must act in response to the rhythms of their age. Their genius must be adapted, in a phrase of William James's, "to the receptivities of the moment." Leaders are useless without followers. "There goes the mob," said the French politician hearing a clamor in the streets. "I am their leader. I must follow them." Great leaders turn the inchoate emotions of the mob to purposes of their own. They seize on the opportunities of their time, the hopes, fears, frustrations, crises, potentialities. They succeed when events have prepared the way for them, when the community is awaiting to be aroused, when they can provide the clarifying and organizing ideas. Leadership ignites the circuit between the individual and the mass and thereby alters history.

It may alter history for better or for worse. Leaders have been responsible for the most extravagant follies and most monstrous crimes that have beset suffering humanity. They have also been vital in such gains as humanity has made in individual freedom, religious and racial tolerance, social justice and respect for human rights.

There is no sure way to tell in advance who is going to lead for good and who for evil. But a glance at the gallery of men and women in *World Leaders—Past and Present* suggests some useful tests.

One test is this: do leaders lead by force or by persuasion? By command or by consent? Through most of history leadership was exercised by the divine right of authority. The duty of followers was to defer and to obey. "Theirs not to reason why,/ Theirs but to do and die." On occasion, as with the so-called "enlightened despots" of the 18th century in Europe, absolutist leadership was animated by humane purposes. More often, absolutism nourished the passion for domination, land, gold and conquest and resulted in tyranny.

The great revolution of modern times has been the revolution of equality. The idea that all people should be equal in their legal condition has undermined the old structure of authority, hierarchy and deference. The revolution of equality has had two contrary effects on the nature of leadership. For equality, as Alexis de Tocqueville pointed out in his great study *Democracy in America*, might mean equality in servitude as well as equality in freedom.

"I know of only two methods of establishing equality in the political world," Tocqueville wrote. "Rights must be given to every citizen, or none at all to anyone . . . save one, who is the master of all." There was no middle ground "between the sovereignty of all and the absolute power of one man." In his astonishing prediction of 20th-century totalitarian dictatorship, Tocqueville explained how the revolution of equality could lead to the *"Führerprinzip"* and more terrible absolutism than the world had ever known.

But when rights are given to every citizen and the sovereignty of all is established, the problem of leadership takes a new form, becomes more exacting than ever before. It is easy to issue commands and enforce them by the rope and the stake, the concentration camp and the *gulag*. It is much harder to use argument and achievement to overcome opposition and win consent. The Founding Fathers of the United States understood the difficulty. They believed that history had given them the opportunity to decide, as Alexander Hamilton wrote in the first Federalist Paper, whether men are indeed capable of basing government on "reflection and choice, or whether they are forever destined to depend . . . on accident and force."

Government by reflection and choice called for a new style of leadership and a new quality of followership. It required leaders to be responsive to popular concerns, and it required followers to be active and informed participants in the process. Democracy does not eliminate emotion from politics; sometimes it fosters demagoguery; but it is confident that, as the greatest of democratic leaders put it, you cannot fool all of the people all of the time. It measures leadership by results and retires those who overreach or falter or fail.

It is true that in the long run despots are measured by results too. But they can postpone the day of judgment, sometimes indefinitely, and in the meantime they can do infinite harm. It is also true that democracy is no guarantee of virtue and intelligence in government, for the voice of the people is not necessarily the voice of God. But democracy, by assuring the right of opposition, offers built-in resistance to the evils inherent in absolutism. As the theologian Reinhold Niebuhr summed it up, "Man's capacity for justice makes democracy possible, but man's inclination to injustice makes democracy necessary."

A second test for leadership is the end for which power is sought. When leaders have as their goal the supremacy of a master race or the promotion of totalitarian revolution or the acquisition and exploitation of colonies or the protection of greed and privilege or the preservation of personal power, it is likely that their leadership will do little to advance the cause of humanity. When their goal is the abolition of slavery, the liberation of women, the enlargement of opportunity for the poor and powerless, the extension of equal rights to racial minorities, the defense of the freedoms of expression and opposition, it is likely that their leadership will increase the sum of human liberty and welfare.

Leaders have done great harm to the world. They have also conferred great benefits. You will find both sorts in this series. Even "good" leaders must be regarded with a certain wariness. Leaders are not demigods; they put on their trousers one leg after another just like ordinary mortals. No leader is infallible, and every leader needs to be reminded of this at regular intervals. Irreverence irritates leaders but is their salvation. Unquestioning submission corrupts leaders and demands followers. Making a cult of a leader is always a mistake. Fortunately hero worship generates its own antidote. "Every hero," said Emerson, "becomes a bore at last."

The signal benefit the great leaders confer is to embolden the rest of us to live according to our own best selves, to be active, insistent, and resolute in affirming our own sense of things. For great leaders attest to the reality of human freedom against the supposed inevitabilities of history. And they attest to the wisdom and power that may lie within the most unlikely of us, which is why Abraham Lincoln remains the supreme example of great leadership. A great leader, said Emerson, exhibits new possibilities to all humanity. "We feed on genius. . . . Great men exist that there may be greater men."

Great leaders, in short, justify themselves by emancipating and empowering their followers. So humanity struggles to master its destiny, remembering with Alexis de Tocqueville: "It is true that around every man a fatal circle is traced beyond which he cannot pass; but within the wide verge of that circle he is powerful and free; as it is with man, so with communities."

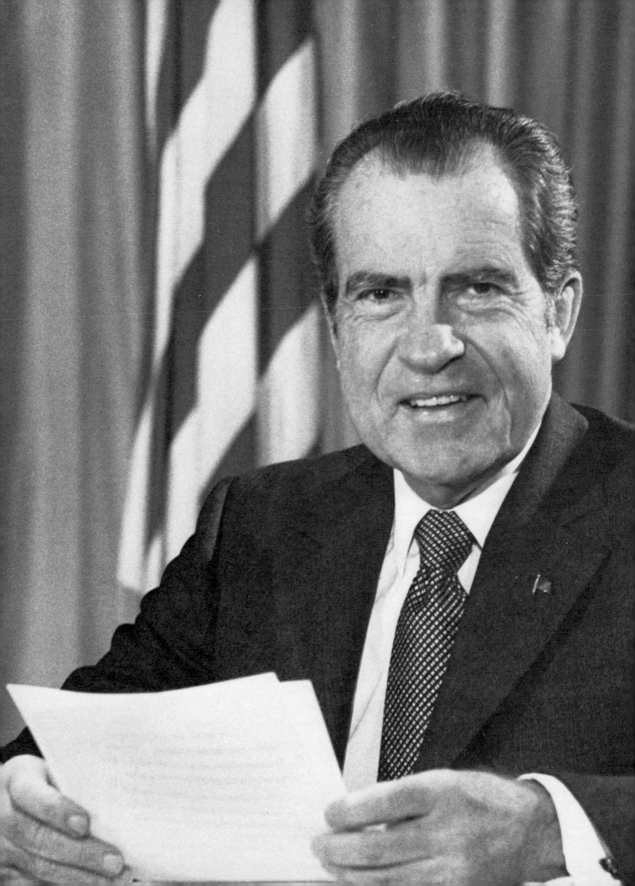

1

The Early Years

America had never before witnessed anything like it. On August 9, 1974, Richard M. Nixon became the first president of the United States to resign from office. After five and one-half years as president and nearly two years of bitter controversy, he assembled his cabinet and White House staff on that August morning to say a personal good-bye to them. Obviously tired and under great strain, his face wet with perspiration, Richard Nixon spoke with emotion and affection. His voice nearly breaking several times, he promised he would see them all again, praised their honesty, and reflected upon his career and on his family, particularly his mother, whom he described as a "saint." Although obviously upset, he insisted he was in "high spirits" and with that left the White House, as a private citizen.

The high drama that drove Nixon from the presidency began two years earlier, during his 1972 reelection campaign. A majority of Americans believed that Nixon had been a good president during his first term; his reelection seemed certain. Nixon's Republican campaign was well staffed, tightly organized, and better funded than any in history. The Democratic challenge was weak. The party was deeply divided, leaving the campaign of candidate George McGovern poorly run, chronically short of money, and thoroughly unprepared for the contest. All the polls and projections predicted a landslide victory for Nixon, perhaps the largest in American history.

This was the first time in history that both the president and vice-president polluted and desecrated their high positions of trust and public confidence.
—WILLIAM O. DOUGLAS
Supreme Court justice, on the Watergate scandal

Richard Nixon, president of the United States, outlines his administration's response to the energy crisis on January 23, 1974. Less than seven months later, facing almost certain impeachment, he became the first American president to resign from office.

UPI/BETTMANN NEWSPHOTOS

THE IMPEACHMENT REPORT

★ ★ ★

A GUIDE TO
CONGRESSIONAL PROCEEDINGS
IN THE CASE OF
RICHARD M. NIXON,
PRESIDENT OF THE UNITED STATES

THE ARTICLES OF IMPEACHMENT
AS RECOMMENDED BY
THE HOUSE JUDICIARY COMMITTEE,
PETER W. RODINO, JR.,
CHAIRMAN

The impeachment report of the House Judiciary Committee recommended that the full House of Representatives vote on whether to bring three charges against Nixon: obstruction of justice, abuse of presidential power, and refusal to obey congressional subpoenas.

Despite such promising circumstances, the Committee to Reelect the President (CREEP) and members of the White House staff engaged in shadowy campaign activities. On June 17, 1972, agents for CREEP unlawfully entered the Democratic National Committee headquarters in the Watergate office building in Washington, D.C. Armed with burglary tools, miniature cameras, and sophisticated electronic equipment, they photographed documents, tapped telephones, and planted listening devices so they might spy on McGovern's troubled presidential campaign. The burglars were caught and arrested but refused to tell authorities why they were in the offices or who had sent them.

The June break-in had no effect on the president's overwhelming reelection victory; the news story was at first largely ignored by the public. The story behind the break-in was revealed, piece by piece, only after months of investigation by newspaper reporters, Justice Department lawyers, special prosecutors, grand juries, and congressional committees. Probes into the Watergate burglary unearthed revelations of corrupt practices and unlawful activities by members of Nixon's staff and a former cabinet member that went far beyond the break-in. The Watergate scandal ultimately encompassed illegal campaign contributions, influence peddling, other burglaries, bribery, perjury, obstruction of justice, and spying on political enemies — all unveiled through the investigation of what appeared initially to be a simple office burglary.

By August 1974 the House of Representatives was poised to vote on a bill of impeachment against the president of the United States. Nixon was charged with "using the power of his high office . . . to delay, impede, and obstruct the investigation" into the Watergate break-in and "to cover up, conceal, and

The House Judiciary Committee met in July 1974 to discuss Nixon's impeachment. It marked only the second time that Congress had debated the bringing of charges against a president. Andrew Johnson was impeached in 1868 but was acquitted in the Senate by only one vote.

protect those responsible; and to conceal . . . other unlawful . . . activities." Under the Constitution, should the full House charge him with "high crimes and misdemeanors" for obstructing justice, misusing federal agencies, and contempt of Congress, the president would have to defend himself before the Senate, which would pass judgment on his innocence or guilt.

Watergate revelations, speculation about the fate of the president, and concern about the scandal's ramifications on the country as a whole became a national obsession that spilled over into the very fiber of American life. Watergate filled the daily newspapers, the evening news, and the casual conversations of ordinary citizens. Congressional hearings were broadcast on daily television during the summer of 1973. All over America people brought radios to their offices and listened to heated accusations and evasive answers.

Congress and the courts investigated allegations of illegal and unethical activities inside the Nixon administration, but the president fought them at every turn. The legal and political issues brought on by Watergate created a constitutional crisis as Nixon, claiming the privilege of the executive branch, refused to cooperate with Congress and the judiciary.

In July 1974 the impasse broke. New evidence provided conclusive proof that Nixon was deeply involved in covering up the break-in and guilty of obstructing justice. There was no longer any doubt that the president had broken laws and betrayed the national trust. Even the president's most loyal supporters told him that he could not survive the impeachment process. They concluded that resignation was the best course of action for Nixon, for the office of the presidency, and for the well-being of the nation.

After his resignation, Nixon and his wife, Pat (center right), leave the White House, escorted by the new president and first lady, Gerald and Betty Ford. One month later Ford unconditionally pardoned Nixon for all crimes he may have committed while in office.

The president never admitted guilt or wrongdoing. He left office with a simple statement: "I hereby resign the Office of President of the United States." In his televised farewell address, Nixon reminded the nation that he had made the world a safer place by ending the long and costly war in Vietnam, by easing tensions with the Soviet Union, and by normalizing diplomatic relations with China. Without referring directly to Watergate, he acknowledged some "wrong" judgments but insisted that he was resigning because he lacked a "strong enough political base in Congress" to prevent impeachment, not because he was guilty of impeachable offenses. For Nixon, ever the politician, Watergate was a matter of votes, not a matter of law or morality, as it had become for the rest of the nation.

His farewell at the White House was dramatic and emotional but revealed nothing about his role in the Watergate scandals. He exited the White House to a standing ovation and boarded a waiting helicopter that took him to the presidential jet for the trip to California and private life after a political career of 28 years.

Nixon was born in 1913 in this newly built house in Yorba Linda, California. When he was nine the family moved to the small, predominantly Quaker community of Whittier, where the family owned and operated a general store.

NATIONAL ARCHIVES

The Nixon family in 1916. At rear are parents Frank and Hannah. In front are brothers Harold (left) and Donald (center). Richard is at right.

It was fitting that Nixon should leave Washington for California, for it is in California that it all began. If the American political tradition prizes humble origins, particularly for its presidents, then Nixon's formative years in California prepared him well for a career in politics. When Richard was born in 1913 in Yorba Linda, his unemployed father, Frank, was investing his efforts in a lemon grove, which eventually failed. Thereafter, Frank Nixon made a living as a carpenter and owner of a small combination general store and gas station in Whittier, where the Nixons moved in 1922. The kindest observers remembered him as a tough, unpredictable, hot-tempered man who was a rough disciplinarian with his children. Richard was the favorite of his mother, Hannah, who raised the five Nixon boys in her Quaker faith and was by all accounts a kind, gentle, long-suffering woman. One of her sons, Arthur, died young; she nursed another, Harold, for several years before he died of tuberculosis. Harold's illness drained the family emotionally and financially.

A solemn Nixon as he appeared as a senior in his high school yearbook. He was an extremely serious and hardworking young man who spent very long hours working in the family store and studying.

The future president was an active and ambitious student at Whittier High School. He worked long hours at the family store, often rising before dawn to drive the family truck to market in Los Angeles. He also spent long hours studying and held several high school offices, although, ironically, he was defeated in a bid to become senior class president. At Whittier College, which he entered at age seventeen, he was an undersized and overeager scrub on the football team for four years but failed to earn a letter. He was more successful as a politician. Nixon formed a social club, served as senior class president, and organized a successful campaign to lift a ban on dancing at the Quaker college.

A skilled debater and a serious student, he earned a tuition scholarship to Duke University's law school in Durham, North Carolina. His financial situation forced him to work at the university library and to live in a boarding house that lacked indoor plumbing. His capacity for remaining at his desk for long hours of study earned him the nickname

"Iron Butt," but his hard work paid off. Fellow students elected him president of the Student Bar Association. His mother and grandmother drove cross-country from California to see him graduate third in a class of twenty-five in the spring of 1937.

The qualities that later characterized Nixon the politician were evident during those early years. He impressed teachers with his hardworking ways and his ability to produce "correct" (if morally ambiguous) answers. He was able to quietly master situations and bodies of knowledge and focused his intelligence on competitive arenas, such as debates. He was not considered an intellectual; he was not interested in ideas for their own sake, but he was interested in ideas that helped him win arguments. Debating gave him quickness of thought and taught him how to argue all sides of an issue.

His skill as an organizer and a strategist, more than the force of his intellect or his personality, formed the basis of his leadership. Although respected by his peers for his diligence and abilities, he was not at ease with them; he appeared aloof and distant, even unfriendly and uncomfortable with strangers. He never attracted a large number of friends, yet he earned the loyalty of a small circle of dedicated followers; attracting loyal followers became one of the hallmarks of his political career.

> *I won my share of scholarships, and of speaking and debating prizes in school, not because I was smarter but because I worked longer and harder than some of my gifted colleagues.*
> —RICHARD NIXON
> on his days at Whittier College

Nixon (back row, third from right) at Duke University Law School. Although he graduated third in his class, Nixon was unable to land a job with a prestigious New York law firm and returned to California to begin his career.

UPI/BETTMANN NEWSPHOTOS

With his new law degree, an ambitious Nixon hoped to join a prestigious New York law firm, but his single interview at one of their oak-paneled offices brought no offer of employment. Nor did the Federal Bureau of Investigation (FBI) accept his services as an agent. So instead of moving up the eastern seaboard, he returned west, back to California.

Nixon returned to the Quaker community of Whittier, with its orange and avocado groves and its unpretentious homes and social climate. He established himself as a competent local attorney and took a turn at business, which proved unsuccessful. He met and married Pat Ryan after returning to Whittier. A bright, active woman who worked her way through the University of California at San Diego as a salesclerk and a walk-on movie actress, she taught at the local high school. Married, practicing law, a leader of local civic and religious organizations, and a trustee of Whittier College at age 26, Nixon gave the appearance of settling down.

The Japanese attacked the U.S. fleet at Pearl Harbor on December 7, 1941, precipitating the United States' entrance into World War II. Raised a Quaker, Nixon rejected the faith's pacifist beliefs by enlisting in the navy.

NATIONAL ARCHIVES

Whittier offered Nixon a place to return to, but it did not satisfy him. He was an extremely ambitious, competitive, and restless man in a small, quiet California town during the depression years of the late 1930s. He remained eager for other things, other places, particularly for the success of a big-city law practice. He had no vision of himself as a politician yet, certainly not as president, but he, as well as his friends and teachers, expected big things of Richard Nixon the lawyer.

World War II provided a way out. After the United States declared war on Japan and Germany in 1941, Nixon went to Washington, D.C. Out of respect for his mother's Quaker pacifist sentiment, he did not immediately enlist in the military service but spent time in the swollen wartime bureaucracy at the Office of Price Administration (OPA). Nixon recalled that his six months with the OPA influenced his political philosophy by convincing him that government tried to do more than was possible for it to do well. He became disillusioned with the bureaucracy — the paperwork, the political appointees who sought power, and the civil servants who, he concluded, lacked passion for their responsibilities. Considering himself a liberal during college, he reported that his first stint in Washington made him more conservative.

After six months in Washington, he enlisted in the navy as a lieutenant junior grade. He served in supply and transport, spending most of his time on Green Island in the South Pacific, which saw no actual combat. Service friends remembered "Nick," as he was known in the military, for two reasons. As a supply officer, he had access to food and other goods not part of military rations, which he dispensed to the men, apparently at no charge. He also earned a reputation as the best poker player on the island, a matter of some importance at a dull outpost of the war where the daily poker game was a major part of military life. At the end of the war Nixon left the service with the rank of lieutenant commander and the ambition of becoming a better and more successful attorney. Within a year, he was running for the U.S. Congress.

In World War II Nixon was an operations officer who earned the rank of lieutenant commander. He saw no action and later envied the genuine war heroism of his political adversary, John F. Kennedy.

2

The Road to Success

In 1945 Richard Nixon was one of thousands of American GIs waiting to be discharged from military service. World War II was ending at last, and Nixon, like the rest of the country, rejoiced at the approaching peace and looked to the future with great enthusiasm and high expectations.

Neither Nixon nor the nation was disappointed. Both found opportunity and success in the postwar years. The war had been a desperately needed shot in the arm to an American economy ravaged by the Great Depression. America's industrial recovery enabled the United States to bolster war-ravaged Europe and Japan with humanitarian aid, reindustrialization, and military protection. At the same time, such overseas aid programs enabled America to continue its economic growth. America grew rich and powerful and secure in its ever-expanding leadership role in the Western world. A 33-year-old Nixon was elected to the U.S. House of Representatives in 1946. Within two years he emerged as a political celebrity for his anticommunist activities. In 1950 he was elected to the United States Senate, and in 1952 Richard Nixon was the 39-year-old vice-president to Republican President Dwight D. Eisenhower. Nixon's road to success was short and smooth.

My strong point, if I have a strong point, is performance. I always produce more than I promise.
—RICHARD NIXON

As a first-term member of the House of Representatives in 1947, Nixon angled for an appointment to the House Un-American Activities Committee (HUAC). Nixon quickly realized that anticommunism was a sure route to political prominence in the postwar United States.

NATIONAL ARCHIVES

He had entered politics by invitation. In the late spring of 1945 a group of influential Republicans from Nixon's district in California met to discuss the upcoming elections. Their first choice as a candidate to seek the district's seat in the House of Representatives declined to run but suggested Nixon as a possible alternative. Additional inquiries convinced the committee that Nixon would be a good candidate to run against five-term Democrat Jerry Voorhis.

Voorhis was a successful congressman from a well-known California family. He took care of his constituents and had the respect of his colleagues in the House. He also had a record as an independent politician who, in the depression years of the 1930s, had demonstrated great tolerance for reform-minded plans aimed at correcting America's economic hard times and easing the suffering of her citizens. He once described himself as a "Christian Socialist" whose favorite programs had become part of the New Deal, as the domestic reform and recovery program of President Franklin D. Roosevelt was known.

American and Soviet soldiers clasp hands at Torgau, Germany, on May 3, 1945. Their armies had jointly liberated Europe from Nazi domination, yet in the postwar years it was the Soviet Union and communism, not fascism, that was perceived as the greatest threat to U.S. interests.

Nixon, his advisers, and the California Republican party recognized that a young, unknown candidate who lacked political experience would have a hard time defeating Voorhis, so they organized a campaign based on the belief that America would become increasingly conservative in the postwar years. A growing national concern with communism was a predominant characteristic of this shift in political values. By 1946 the wartime alliance between the Soviet Union and the United States had given way to the cold war, a period of intense rivalry and suspicion between the two nations that influenced every aspect of American life, especially politics. The American people watched anxiously as several Eastern European countries became communist, under the direct influence of the Soviet Union contrary to wartime agreements that had been made between the United States and Russia. Americans came to fear that communism would spread uncontrollably and eventually threaten the security of the United States, either directly or by subversive activities by communist agents or sympathizers at home. Nixon understood early in his political life that candidates who could be tainted with the communist label—accurately or not—faced near certain defeat, and Nixon skillfully and shamelessly built his career on that understanding.

Nixon (right) with HUAC's special counsel Robert Stripling (center) and John McDowell, another committee member. The anticommunism movement initially focused on alleged espionage within the government; later the crusade investigated subversion in the arts, education, and other areas of society.

Hallie Flanagan, director of the Federal Theatre Project, part of FDR's New Deal, testifies in 1938 before a Congressional committee investigating communist subversion. The widespread suffering during the Great Depression of the 1930s led many Americans to question the justness of capitalism.

While America's preoccupation with cold war politics made the domestic climate ripe for tactics such as Nixon's, the anticommunism of the period also has its roots in the almost total collapse of the American economy in the late 1920s and early 1930s known as the Great Depression. The unprecedented (for the United States) economic devastation wrought by the depression, with its consequent toll in human misery and suffering, led many Americans — intellectuals, artists, politicians, educators, workers — to question the political and economic institutions of the United States. Many were drawn to communism and socialism. The American capitalist system, it was argued, was inherently inequitable and led inevitably to collapses such as the depression. Communism, theoretically, distributed the wealth more fairly. In the early days of the depression, before Roosevelt's recovery programs had an effect, it was widely felt that the government was indifferent to the suffering of its citizens. Many looked to the Soviet Union, the world's only communist state, as a model of enlightened social leadership. (At the time, little was known about the abuses of the Stalin regime, its totalitarian nature, or the later duplicitous Soviet foreign policy.) The

Soviet Union was also initially seen as the leader in the fight against fascism — the same facism against which the United States would wage World War II — by virtue of its aid to republican Spain during the Spanish civil war. So when Nixon and others initiated the anticommunist crusade, they found that many Americans had flirted with communism.

Of all the House of Representatives seats that were contested in 1946, the Nixon-Voorhis race was perhaps the nastiest. Always the hard worker, Nixon proved to be a tireless and vigorous candidate who involved himself in every aspect of the campaign. As the election progressed, he and his staff focused on two issues that moved Nixon toward victory. First was Nixon's war record. Although he exaggerated his combat experience (he had none but regularly spoke about defending his country in "the mud and stinking jungles" of the South Pacific), he nevertheless had the edge on Voorhis, who had served in Congress during the war. Second, and most important, Nixon convinced many voters that Voorhis was backed by communists and, by implication, was perhaps one himself, although there was no evidence to support either charge. During the campaign Voorhis was accused of voting "the Moscow line" in Congress, and at Republican headquarters employees called voters, asking, "Did you know Jerry Voorhis is a communist?" Nixon's skill at keeping Voorhis on the defensive about the communism issue helped elect him to his first political office.

Nixon's early service in the House of Representatives was typical for most first-termers — a lot of hard work and not much accomplished, except for his membership on the House Committee on Un-American Activities. He also sat on the Labor Committee. He teamed up with a fellow member, Charles Kersten of Wisconsin, to study the communism problem. Kersten introduced Nixon to Father John Cronin of the National Catholic Welfare Conference, who through investigation of communist infiltration of labor unions, had become something of an expert on communism. Nixon, like many others, was convinced by Father Cronin that there were

Two of the "Hollywood Ten," members of the film industry who were convicted of contempt for refusing to cooperate with the HUAC, on their way to jail in 1950. Witnesses were often pressured to name other suspected communists.

In 1948 Whittaker Chambers (pictured) accused Alger Hiss, a former State Department official, of passing confidential government information to the Soviet Union. Nixon's tenacity in pursuing the case thrust him into the national spotlight.

UPI/BETTMANN NEWSPHOTOS

communists operating in atomic espionage rings and in the State Department. The House Committee on Un-American Activities, also known as HUAC, was given the responsibility of investigating America's enemies at home. Late in Nixon's first term, the committee began a series of hearings aimed at identifying communist spies and sympathizers, with a special emphasis on locating any that might be in government service.

The committee heard public testimony from witnesses suspected of having useful information. The growing fear of communism generated by the cold war and the promise of spectacular revelations about spies and traitors attracted attention in Washington and in the nationwide media.

Despite the press attention and the excitement, the committee had produced no positive results by the summer of 1948. There was a growing feeling that the hearings were becoming an embarrassment to the Congress and the nation. Critics of the committee, including Democratic President Harry S. Truman, argued that the hearings were a failure and should be ended.

Into this debate stepped three main players: committee member Richard M. Nixon, former Communist party member Whittaker Chambers, and Alger Hiss, a former foreign policy coordinator with the State Department, well known and respected in government circles and a friend of many powerful citizens.

Chambers, once a senior editor of *Time* magazine, reported to the committee that Hiss was a member of the Communist party. The statement caused a sensation. Hiss came before the committee to deny the charges. With his background of Harvard Law School, secretary to Supreme Court Justice Oliver Wendell Holmes, adviser to the United Nations, president of the prestigious Carnegie Endowment for International Peace, Hiss was unlike other witnesses heard by the committee. His reputation and his polished, poised testimony swayed the committee and most of the nation. It looked for a time as if the charges made against Hiss might be the committee's final embarrassment.

Alger Hiss's Ivy League education and membership in the so-called Eastern political establishment differed greatly from Nixon's background. Nixon wrote that Hiss "was too suave, too smooth, and too self-confident to be an entirely trustworthy witness."

Nixon was not convinced. He took on the Hiss case as a crusade. Nixon interviewed Chambers for countless hours and slowly brought together enough information, including copies of government documents that Hiss was said to have passed to the Soviets through Chambers, to keep the Hiss case before the committee and the nation. After months of public debate and controversy and the revelation of a second, more damaging set of documents known as the "Pumpkin Papers" (Hiss was alleged to have hid microfilmed documents in a pumpkin patch), Hiss was charged in federal court with perjury for having lied to the committee. When the first trial — based almost exclusively on Chambers's testimony — ended in a hung jury, Nixon accused the presiding judge of being prejudiced in

31

Hiss's favor and demanded another trial. At the second trial, Hiss was found guilty of perjury for having told the committee he had not passed any government documents to Chambers. After 44 months in prison, Hiss was released on parole and dropped out of public view, working as a stationery and printing-supplies salesman in New York. He periodically tried to clear his name and was readmitted to the Massachusetts bar in 1975. Hiss's innocence or guilt and Nixon's role in the Hiss case is a matter of continued debate among historians.

The Hiss case was perfect for the times and for Nixon's political career. Out of America's cold war fears came a nervous search for domestic enemies, a search that found expression in the HUAC hearings and Nixon's investigation of Alger Hiss. Nixon's persistence in such a well-publicized and dramatic

Helen Gahagan Douglas campaigns for election to the Senate in 1950. Nixon's campaign against her was one of the dirtiest in California history. Douglas gave him the nickname that stuck throughout his political career—"Tricky Dick."

case transformed him from an obscure California congressman into a national public figure whom many viewed as a hero. It also moved Nixon into the front ranks of young Republican leaders. At a time when each political party was seeking to convince the voters that it was more anticommunist than the other party, Nixon earned that title for the Republicans. In return, Nixon's rise to prominence continued long after the Hiss case ended, and he became the Republican's best-known standard bearer in the cold war struggle.

Nixon's ambitions kept pace with his rising reputation. He won both the Democratic and Republican nomination for reelection to his House seat in 1948, and although friends and advisers cautioned him against any reckless career decisions, he chose to run for the U.S. Senate in 1950. As he faced Congresswoman Helen Gahagan Douglas, he did not forget what he had learned from the Voorhis campaign and the Hiss case — anticommunism was popular, made headlines, and put opponents on the defensive.

The Nixon-Douglas battle is remembered as one of the dirtiest in modern political history. There were genuine issues in 1950, for America and for California. The wartime economic boom was giving way to a recession, fighting had broken out in Korea, Europe continued to struggle with postwar recovery, and corruption was the favorite topic of gossip in Washington.

Subversion and communist activity also played a role in almost every other election in the fall of 1950, but in no other race did it play such an important role. Nixon and his campaign people made it the main issue in his race for the Senate. Time after time, in speech after speech, Nixon insisted that Douglas had a "soft attitude toward communists" and that her votes in Congress threatened the security of the United States and aided the communist conspiracy in America. Nixon asked why she had "followed the communist line so many times" and accused her of giving "comfort to Soviet tyranny." The election, concluded Nixon, was "simply a choice between freedom and state socialism."

If the American people understood the real character of Alger Hiss, they would boil him in oil.
—RICHARD NIXON

UPI/BETTMANN NEWSPHOTOS

Nixon, the Republican vice-presidential candidate, meets young Republicans in Washington, D.C., in 1952. At 39, he was the second-youngest vice-president ever elected.

Nixon's tactics were epitomized by his branding Mrs. Douglas the "Pink Lady" (a reference to her supposed connections with communists, who were sometimes called "pinkos" or "Reds") and then circulating 500,000 copies of a bright pink leaflet called the pink sheet. It was presented as an authentic list of votes cast by Douglas in Congress, votes that supposedly supported un-American activities and thereby hurt national security.

The Nixon tactics worked. Churches, newspapers, and anti-Semitic organizations joined traditional Republican and patriotic groups to accuse Douglas of being procommunist and unfit for the Senate. Late in the campaign a *Los Angeles Times* editorial described her as "the darling of the Hollywood parlor pinks and Reds" and insisted that she had "voted the Communist party line in Congress innumerable times."

Nixon knew that none of the charges were true, but his main concern was whether the communism issue could get him elected to the Senate. His answer came on election day when he won with a surprising 680,000-vote margin.

The California Senate race and the earlier Hiss case made Nixon the best-known new member of the Senate in 1951. His reputation as an anticommunist and his aggressive, name-calling campaign style earned him more speaking invitations than he could manage, but he accepted all that his schedule would allow — campaigning for other Republicans seeking office, lecturing on the communist conspiracy, attacking the Democrats, and promising audiences a brighter future with the Republicans.

As the presidential nominating convention of 1952 drew near, Nixon was the most prominent young star of the Republican party. His supporters talked about the impressive list of achievements he had crowded into a brief political career. Young, tough, and articulate, a brilliant campaigner, the most sought-after Republican speaker, an ardent anticommunist with experience in both the House of Representatives and the Senate, Nixon was an ideal vice-presidential candidate. The Republican delegates to the presidential nominating convention in 1952 agreed. They selected Dwight D. Eisenhower, general of the army and supreme allied commander in Europe in World War II, as their candidate for president and Richard Nixon for vice-president.

He had come a long way in seven years. In 1945 he had been a small-town lawyer, one of many thousands of recently discharged veterans returning to their prewar lives. That year he discussed a political future with a group of influential local Republicans. By 1952 he was Senator Nixon, crisscrossing the nation as the vice-presidential candidate on a ticket with General Eisenhower, the nation's hero from World War II and the man who most observers believed would be elected president in the fall.

> *If the dry rot of corruption and communism, which has eaten deep into our body politic during the past seven years, can only be chopped out with a hatchet — then let's call for a hatchet.*
> —RICHARD NIXON
> 1952

3

Grand Ambitions, Great Disappointments

Within a week of starting his campaign for the vice-presidency in September 1952, Nixon became involved in a controversy so intense that it looked as though he might be asked to resign from the ticket. The Republicans had made corruption a major campaign issue in 1952. Nixon and Eisenhower's "Crusade for Political Purity," as they called it, promised to drive the "Democratic crooks" out of office and to bring an "Honest Deal" to the American people. The charge was turned against Nixon, and he was accused in print of having a secret slush fund for private expenses that had been established in 1950 by wealthy backers eager to support an obvious rising star in the Republican party.

The days following the disclosure were tense ones for Nixon, as the story became the biggest issue of the young campaign. Nixon maintained that the fund was public knowledge, had been used only for campaign expenses, and consisted of small donations solicited by his campaign workers. He was being "smeared," he said, by the "crooks and communists" he had been exposing.

Nixonland is a land of slander and scare . . . the land of push and grab and anything to win.
—ADLAI E. STEVENSON
Democratic candidate for
president, 1952

Nixon is greeted by supporters during his 1952 campaign. Early in the campaign the revelation that Nixon controlled a secret slush fund nearly forced his withdrawal from the ticket.

In Williamstown, Massachusetts, in 1952, the Democratic headquarters cleverly one-upped the campaign slogan of the Republicans, whose headquarters was next door. Known as Ike, Eisenhower was an extremely popular candidate; both parties had sought him as their nominee.

Eager to avoid even the hint of impropriety around the campaign of the enormously popular Eisenhower, Republican party leaders sought Nixon's withdrawal. It appears that Eisenhower himself favored this course, but Nixon resisted several thinly veiled hints of the presidential nominee's desire to see him go.

It was finally agreed that Nixon would take his case to the American people through a nationally televised address, with public opinion to decide his fate. An extremely favorable response to his speech would allow Nixon to remain as the candidate. Four days after the initial news story had appeared, a nervous and anxious Nixon faced the cameras to discuss the origins of the fund and to explain its purpose. He recited his entire financial history as evidence that he had not personally profited from the fund. He assured the audience that he knew, as they did, that what he had accumulated "isn't very much, but Pat and I have the satisfaction of knowing that every dime we have is honestly ours. I should say this," continued Nixon, "that Pat doesn't have a mink coat, but she does have a respectable Republican cloth coat."

There was something else he thought he should tell the people about: a gift. A man in Texas had heard Pat say over the radio that the two Nixon girls would like a puppy, and just after the nomination he had sent them a little black-and-white cocker spaniel. "And our little girl — Tricia, the six-year-old — named it Checkers. And you know, the kids, like all kids, loved the dog; and I just want to say this, right now, that regardless of what they say about it, we are going to keep him."

The Checkers speech, as it became known, was one of Nixon's most effective political moves. The fund disturbed many people because it suggested the questionable ethics of having a public career financed by wealthy men who might seek favors; the fund's alleged secrecy only served to support that sinister interpretation. It gave the appearance that Nixon represented a few powerful and wealthy contributors and that he could be bought. With the Checkers speech Nixon laid open his personal finances to public scrutiny and transformed the issue from the propriety of such funds to whether he had personally profited from its existence. He also challenged the Democratic candidates, Adlai Stevenson and John Sparkman, to make similar financial disclosures.

Nixon with Checkers. In his famous 1952 speech, Nixon admitted accepting the dog as a gift for his children but denied profiting from a slush fund. The televised speech saved Nixon's vice-presidential candidacy.

For the first time, people saw a living political drama on their TV sets — a man fighting for his whole career and future — and they judged him under that strain. It was an even greater achievement than it seemed.

—GARRY WILLS
journalist and historian, on the Checkers speech

The speech, with its homey touches about cloth coats and family pets, convinced the viewers that the fund was for proper political expenses, not personal gain, and that the Nixons were honest people of modest means. Over 300,000 responded to the speech by telephone and telegraph, nearly all in Nixon's favor. Eisenhower told Nixon, "You're my boy." The crisis had passed. The Checkers speech saved Nixon's political career.

Nixon resumed the campaign trail with new energy for the task at hand — defeating the Democrats. While Eisenhower remained aloof from the combative side of the election, Nixon returned to the issue that had served him so well in previous elections — the communist conspiracy. Adlai Stevenson was a perfect foil for Nixon in 1952. Nixon scored points and earned votes by noting that Stevenson had served as a character reference for his old friend Alger Hiss. Stevenson became "Adlai the Appeaser" of communists; the Democrats became the party with a policy of "Cowardly Communist Containment," which was Nixon's way of saying they were soft on communism at home and throughout the world. Eisenhower went to the White House on a campaign pitted against taxes, inflation, corruption, the war in Korea, and communism.

The Nixons and Eisenhowers share the stage at the 1952 Republican convention in Chicago. Eisenhower cultivated a genial, nonpartisan image during the campaign while Nixon hammered away at the Democrats on the issues of corruption and internal subversion.

UPI/BETTMANN NEWSPHOTOS

Nixon became vice-president of the United States at age 39, the second-youngest man ever to hold the office. His rise to power was fueled mostly by his success as an anticommunist and his willingness (and ability) to engage in the nasty, rough-and-tumble side of American politics. Nixon drew on these successes while he was vice-president, but they did not always work to his advantage.

One of Nixon's responsibilities to the party was keeping peace between Senator Joseph McCarthy and the rest of the Republicans. Beginning in 1950, McCarthy, a Republican senator from Wisconsin, directed a relentless campaign against suspected communists. He insisted that there was a widespread communist conspiracy inside America, although none was ever disclosed. He made unfounded charges against countless people, including Hollywood actors and writers, college professors, and foreign-service officers. McCarthy's irresponsible accusations ruined many innocent lives and helped cause a national hysteria that is looked upon today as one of the most shameful periods in American history. Richard Nixon and Joseph McCarthy led the crusade. Other groups took up their cause — finding communists became a national obsession.

Senator Joseph McCarthy (left) and his aide Roy Cohn (right) used irresponsible and unsupported allegations to create a climate of hysteria about communism in which many lives were damaged. McCarthy's influence waned after the Senate condemned him for his tactics in 1954.

41

So powerful was McCarthy that for a time no politician dared challenge him, including President Eisenhower, but he became a problem for his own party. Once the Republicans gained control of the White House in 1952, McCarthy's sensational and fabricated charges about communists in government service became attacks on Eisenhower's administration. Nixon, with his reputation as an anticommunist, was regularly called upon to control the senator from Wisconsin, but as time went on and McCarthy began to run out of control, Nixon had little success as the party peacekeeper.

The two had their differences over style and party loyalty. Nixon saw no value in Republicans accusing Republicans, while McCarthy was a political maverick who became caught up in a drama of his own making — the party was secondary to him. McCarthy went too far in his crusade when he turned his accusations on the Protestant clergy and the U.S. army in March 1954. President Eisenhower denounced him publicly, and the Senate voted to censure him. Nixon's association with the Wisconsin senator hurt him with many Americans, who forever — and correctly — identified Nixon with the excesses of the McCarthy era.

Nixon's other political asset at that time was his combative style — he was known as the guy who would say or do what was necessary to get the job done, the way he had in his early races against Voorhis and Douglas. From the time he went to the Senate in 1950 and campaigned so effectively for other Republican candidates, he earned the reputation as the Republican party's lightning rod, a controversial figure who would come out swinging in support of all Republicans who were running for office.

As vice-president, Nixon hoped for new and substantial responsibilities in the administration, but he found himself excluded from the White House inner circle, with little access to Eisenhower or the major decision-making situations. Yet administration insiders expected Nixon to assume heavy duties during the off-year elections of 1954. The Republicans needed victories in several key Congressional races for the Eisenhower administration to have any hope of seeing its programs enacted. Nixon was given a grueling schedule that had him traveling 26,000 miles in 48 days so he could speak in 95 cities in 31 states on behalf of nearly every Republican candidate. He gave 204 speeches and more than 100 interviews and press conferences.

Nixon gave Eisenhower and the party leaders the hard work they always expected of him. In speech after speech he told voters that the Republican party had thrown thousands of communists out of government jobs and that it was working hard to defeat Democratic "left wing" candidates who, Nixon charged, had the support of the Communist party. Nixon insisted that almost every Democratic candidate running for office was part of the "left-wing clique which has been so blind to the Communist conspiracy and has tolerated it in the United States."

Republicans congratulated Nixon on his "hard-hitting" contribution to so many campaigns. But anticommunism was wearing out as an emotional issue, as indicated by the growing dismay with McCarthy's tactics, and Nixon's tactics failed. The voters gave the Democrats control of both houses of Congress and the governor's chair in seven closely contested states.

As momentum for the presidential election in 1956 began to build, Nixon faced yet another crisis — two attempts to remove him from the Republican ticket. Eisenhower planned to seek reelection but gave every appearance of wanting a new running mate. Eisenhower, in truth, considered Nixon too partisan for such a high office. Also, Nixon's aggressive campaign style and his combative political ways made Eisenhower uncomfortable. Nixon seemed locked into the campaign style and rhetoric of the McCarthy era even though the threat from domestic communists proved to be false and no longer interested the public. There had also been distrust between the two since the slush fund incident in 1952, with Nixon resenting Eisenhower for his initial lack of support and Eisenhower suspicious of the independence Nixon displayed in ignoring his hints to remove himself from the ticket.

Adlai the appeaser . . . got a Ph.D. from Dean Acheson's College of Cowardly Communist Containment.
—RICHARD NIXON
on Adlai Stevenson

Republican leaders also worried that the president's age and health would be issues in 1956, putting the vice-presidential candidate in a special situation — as the next president in the event something happened to Eisenhower. In a situation that called for a statesman, they feared Nixon lacked the proper image.

Nixon survived both attempts to bump him off the ticket. As he had done in 1952, Eisenhower refused to come right out and say that he wanted another running mate, and the party leaders who believed that Nixon's negative image would hurt in the election failed to convince enough influential Republicans that the issue was worth fighting for at the convention. Another crisis passed.

Nixon was shaken by the movements to unseat him. He apparently recognized that the very qualities that brought him success early on — his mudslinging style and his red-baiting — were now hurting his career. He made no mention of it, but Nixon changed his ways during the presidential campaign of 1956. He avoided name-calling and character assaults, and he toned down the unsubstantiated charges about opponents being soft on communism. Even though the Democrats ran Adlai Stevenson for president once again, Nixon resisted the temptation to smear Stevenson with the communist label, as he had in 1952. The Eisenhower-Nixon ticket swept to an easy victory in the November election.

Nixon's second term as vice-president was more successful than his first. Circumstances presented him with a series of challenging situations and events that revealed to the American people and the Republican party a more professional and statesmanlike Richard Nixon.

The failing health of President Eisenhower became a test for the vice-president. Nixon's actions earned him high marks, particularly from the professional politicians. The process of governing must continue even if the president falls seriously ill — there are papers to sign, decisions to make, and meetings to attend — and Nixon was aware that all eyes would be on him to see how he responded. It

Eisenhower recovers after his heart attack in September 1955. Nixon received high marks for his caretaking role during the president's illness but was soon told that Eisenhower no longer wanted him on the 1956 election ticket.

was a difficult situation for the vice-president. If he appeared too eager, too full of a take-charge attitude, he would be accused of usurping the power of the presidency while Eisenhower lay ill. If he held back too much and did not perform essential tasks, he would be accused of being too timid and cautious for such a powerful position. Nearly every observer credited Nixon with acting in the proper fashion. His stock went up with both the public and the party leaders.

During his second term Nixon became the most widely traveled vice-president in history. At the request of the president, Nixon undertook a series of foreign missions — to the Far East, to Latin America, to Africa, and to Russia. He met with world leaders, learned about their national concerns, and received an extensive education in foreign affairs that helped prepare him for the presidency. Nixon later remembered these trips as critical to his development.

Two of the missions produced dramatic events that received international attention and boosted Nixon's reputation and career. One took place in Caracas, Venezuela, and the other in Moscow, Russia.

In 1958 the Nixons took an eight-country tour of Latin America. While in Caracas, they were attacked by a mob. The incident started with a hostile, jeering crowd at the airport, and then later, as the motorcade traveled through the city streets en route to the Panteón and a wreath-laying ceremony, it was swamped by demonstrators. Unable to move in the mass of angry demonstrators, the lead limousine, which carried the vice-president, was rocked and pelted with stones. As flying glass from the smashed windows showered the occupants, U.S. Secret Service agents pulled their loaded revolvers in expectation of the mob breaking into the limousine. Nixon and his party were held captive inside the stalled automobile until the truck carrying reporters ahead of the car broke free of the traffic jam and cleared a path for the motorcade. Abandoning the agenda, the Nixons went directly to the American embassy. The mobs spread through the city, and

Nixon meets Cuba's premier, Fidel Castro, in Washington in 1959. Nixon believed his knowledge of foreign affairs to be his greatest asset; he considered his many trips abroad and meetings with foreign leaders while vice-president invaluable learning experiences.

GO AWAY NIXON

DIPLOMACY

N DE U.S.A.

GO HOME

even after the Nixons reached the embassy, their safety was not guaranteed. It looked for a time as if the riots might bring down the government.

While the Nixons remained inside the embassy, sketchy and alarmed reports of events in Caracas reached the news media and Washington. Uncertain of the situation, Eisenhower readied a detachment of U.S. troops to rescue the Nixons should it come to that. At the embassy, Nixon canceled all outside appointments; the building was surrounded by the Venezuelan army, while U.S. Marines and Secret Service men patrolled the corridors inside.

Early the following day, Eisenhower made telephone contact with Nixon at the embassy. A relieved president informed Nixon that the world had followed the dangerous events at Caracas, and he joined in a chorus of universal praise and admiration for Nixon's courage and fortitude, heady praise from the man who had soldiered on most of the European battlefields of World War II.

Jeering crowds greeted the arrival of the Nixons in Caracas, Venezuela, for a goodwill visit in May 1958. Eisenhower sent U.S. ships to Venezuela to ensure Nixon's safety; his actions further angered the Venezuelans, who resented U.S. intervention in their nation's affairs.

The Nixons returned to Washington to a hero's welcome. They were greeted at the airport by President Eisenhower, the cabinet, a congressional delegation, and thousands of well-wishers. Nixon hoped that the genuine upsurge in his popularity after the ordeal in Caracas would earn him the reputation as a man of grace and courage under fire.

A year later Nixon faced a hostile confrontation of another sort. He journeyed to Moscow, the capital of the Soviet Union, to conduct a goodwill tour, to meet with Soviet leader Nikita Khrushchev, and to open an exhibition of American consumer goods. On the day the exhibition began Nixon and Khrushchev engaged in far-reaching and sometimes heated discussions about a variety of subjects — dishwashers, women's rights, workers' housing, capitalism, and nuclear war, among them — as they

Nixon (center) debated Soviet premier Nikita Khrushchev (front, third from left) at an exhibition of American goods in Moscow in 1959. The so-called kitchen debate stamped Nixon as a staunch cold warrior, ensuring his nomination for president in 1960.

UPI/BETTMANN NEWSPHOTOS

walked through the exhibition hall filled with American products.

Khrushchev, a tough and aggressive ex-miner, tended to bully people as a way of taking their measure. Nixon was up to it. He contested Khrushchev on every point, and once — while standing in the middle of a model American kitchen — Nixon poked his finger at Khrushchev's chest for emphasis; a photographer captured the scene. The day-long discussion became known as the "kitchen debate."

News stories about the debate and the accompanying photo of the determined Nixon were widely circulated; they made Nixon an international celebrity and renewed his status as a symbol of resistance to communism. The incident earned Nixon the cover of *Life* magazine and generous treatment by nearly all American news publications.

It also moved him closer to the Republican nomination for president in 1960. Nixon seemed the certain nominee. He had made peace with other potential candidates and was the heir-apparent to the Eisenhower years, so by the time the delegates met in Chicago in July 1960, Nixon was in charge. The convention went as planned. He was nominated for president, and Henry Cabot Lodge of Massachusetts, former senator and U.N. representative, was selected as his running mate. The main theme of the platform was the threat of communist expansion throughout the world and the need for mature and experienced leadership to combat it. Nixon promised to continue the programs of the Eisenhower years.

The Democrats ran John F. Kennedy, the two-term senator from Massachusetts. Lyndon B. Johnson, Senate majority leader from Texas, who was at one time a leading contender for the top spot, rounded out the ticket.

Kennedy was handsome, wealthy, well educated, a genuine war hero, and a prize-winning author. He promised to be a tough opponent for Nixon. Kennedy brought to the campaign a well-financed and sophisticated political organization that had been seasoned by several hard-fought primary battles. Kennedy also had several liabilities. He was only 43

> *You don't know anything about communism — except fear.*
> —NIKITA S. KHRUSHCHEV
> Soviet premier, to Richard Nixon

49

years old, had little administrative experience, and possessed an undistinguished record in the Senate. Most critical, he was a Roman Catholic at a time when it was widely believed that a Catholic could never be elected president.

Nixon went into the campaign with confidence. He was organized, experienced, well known, and the logical successor to Eisenhower, one of the nation's best-loved and most respected leaders. Nixon also had an early poll that showed him leading Kennedy by a comfortable margin.

The election campaign had three critical moments. One hinged on religion, one on race, and one on television.

Nixon avoided using Kennedy's religion as a campaign issue out of fear that it would backfire. He was confident that it would be raised by other people, which it was. Kennedy defused the issue by facing it directly at the first appropriate opportunity. When a group of prominent Protestant leaders (who feared that a Catholic president might take orders directly from the pope in Rome) published a manifesto on the religion question, Kennedy replied with a major address in Houston, Texas. His detailed and thorough response to the manifesto included an unequivocal statement favoring a

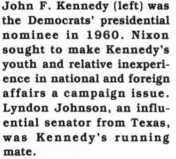

John F. Kennedy (left) was the Democrats' presidential nominee in 1960. Nixon sought to make Kennedy's youth and relative inexperience in national and foreign affairs a campaign issue. Lyndon Johnson, an influential senator from Texas, was Kennedy's running mate.

SMITHSONIAN

complete separation of church and state. After the Houston speech, religion was no longer an issue with most people, except for religious bigots and Ku Klux Klan groups, who had little impact on the election.

If religion was Kennedy's problem in 1960, race was Nixon's. Just weeks before the election, civil rights leader Reverend Martin Luther King, Jr., was sentenced to a prison term of hard labor after being arrested during a sit-in at an Atlanta department store. There was a genuine concern that the controversial civil rights leader would be killed if he was sent to the hard-labor prison. When news of the harsh sentence became public, Kennedy responded

In his first televised debate with Nixon in 1960, Kennedy emerged the clear winner. The younger man appeared confident, knowledgeable, and relaxed. Nixon, who had used television so effectively for the Checkers speech, seemed ill at ease, defensive, and unprepared.

51

immediately. He called King's wife to express his concern and then used his influence to get Reverend King released on bail while an appeal was filed. Nixon remained silent. Kennedy's action and Nixon's hesitancy quickened a significant shift of black voters to Kennedy that probably was the decisive factor in several states.

But the 1960 election is best remembered because it was the first time candidates debated on live television. This, too, became Nixon's burden. The first debate was the most important. To millions of viewers Nixon appeared tired, haggard, ill at ease, defensive, and perspiring and nervous (much the way he was when he said good-bye to the White House staff 14 years later). Worse yet, he seemed unprepared, ill informed, and uncertain of himself. In contrast, Kennedy—tanned and healthy looking—came across as poised, confident, self-assured, articulate, and informed — all qualities the viewers wanted in a president.

Nixon did better in the subsequent debate, but people remembered their first impressions, and they liked what they saw in Kennedy. After the first debate Kennedy's age and maturity stopped being issues. He increased in popularity in the polls, drew larger crowds, and grabbed a handful of key endorsements. The televised debates were one of the most important factors in the campaign.

The election was very close. Nixon lost by a scant 119,450 votes, out of more than 68 million cast, a difference of one-tenth of one percent. The black vote was decisive in five states. There is sound speculation (but no firm evidence) that two states (Texas and Illinois) went to Kennedy through fraud.

When John F. Kennedy took office on a cold, snowy day in January 1961, Richard M. Nixon became a private citizen for the first time in 14 years. He and the family — Pat and teenage daughters Tricia, and Julie — moved back to California, where Nixon joined a law firm, wrote political articles, and, like so many politicians out of office, began work on a book. *Six Crises* relives the major ordeals that Nixon endured: the Hiss case, the slush fund, Eisenhower's illness, the Caracas mob, the Khru-

> *Isn't that a hell of a thing — that the fate of a great country can depend on camera angles?*
> —RICHARD NIXON
> on televised campaign debates

shchev kitchen debate, and the 1960 campaign. Sympathetic readers saw the book as a sympathetic portrait of a world leader who was often misunderstood yet faced each challenge with courage. Others saw early signs of the character flaws that became so pronounced during the difficult days of Watergate. The book sold well and helped restore the defeated candidate's personal and political reputation.

Despite financial success and a busy schedule, Nixon could not resist the lure of politics. He decided to run for governor of California in 1962. Worried friends and advisers cautioned against the move, warning Nixon that he would be accused of wanting the governorship only as a base from which to make another bid for the presidency. They also pointed out that Pat Brown, the incumbent Democrat who was running for reelection, had been a good and popular governor and would be difficult to unseat. More insistent voices convinced Nixon that if he wanted to be president, he needed a strong party organization at home as a stepping-stone, and the governorship of California was made to order. Nixon agreed. His unbridled ambition overruled his political instincts.

The petty, dirty campaign that followed cost both parties a total of nearly $3 million, was void of real issues, and saw Pat Brown reelected in a close vote. In defeat, Nixon, who always prized being in control, lost his temper. As it became clear that he had lost another campaign, this time for a governorship, a humiliated, tired, and angry Nixon met reporters at the Beverly Hilton Hotel. Whining, at times incoherent, Nixon spoke for 15 minutes on a variety of campaign-related subjects, but the press was the real target of his anger. He accused the media of misrepresenting him from the time of the Hiss case and implied that they were deliberately unfair to him. He closed the conference by announcing his retirement from politics: "But as I leave you I want you to know . . . you won't have Nixon to kick around anymore, because, gentlemen, this is my last press conference."

With that, Nixon left the room and electoral politics for six years.

4

"The New Nixon"

Richard Nixon spent from 1963 to 1968 out of office but not outside the political arena. In the spring of 1963 he left California to join a prestigious New York law firm, just the sort he had hoped to impress when he graduated from Duke Law School. He took up residence in New York City, and for a time it appeared he would remain true to the sentiments of his last press conference and stay clear of politics. But the events of the mid-1960s — the assassination of President Kennedy, the doomed presidential candidacy of conservative Republican Barry Goldwater, the deep divisions in the Republican party that followed, the growing racial tensions and violence in the streets, the war in Vietnam, and other turbulent events of the time — drew Nixon back into public life.

After losing the race for governor of California in 1962, the Nixons moved into an expensive apartment in one of New York's fine neighborhoods. Tricia and Julie attended fashionable schools, and when the appropriate time came, each had a debutante ball. The Nixons belonged to the best metropolitan and country clubs and generally led the sort of life expected of a former vice-president with

I believe there really is a 'New Nixon,' a maturer and mellower man who is no longer clawing his way to the top.
—WALTER LIPPMANN
journalist

The Vietnam War was a disturbing experience both for those Americans who fought it and the nation as a whole. Nixon pledged to end the war, but it would be nearly six years before all the American troops were withdrawn.

AP/WIDE WORLD

Nixon with his wife, Pat, and daughters Julie (top left) and Tricia in August 1963. At the time Nixon's political career seemed finished; he had lost elections for president in 1960 and for governor of California in 1962.

a substantial income. Nixon maintained a busy work schedule that included a great deal of international travel and contact with foreign leaders, which gave him a continued claim of expertise in foreign affairs.

Both political parties — like the nation — experienced dramatic changes during the 1960s. On November 22, 1963, President Kennedy was assassinated in Dallas, Texas, and while a shocked nation mourned, Lyndon Johnson became the 36th president of the United States.

Johnson was an active president. His domestic program — called the Great Society — included the ambitious goals of ridding the nation of poverty, illness, ignorance, and racial discrimination. He had legislation enacted in support of federal medical care for the aged, civil rights for black Americans, cleaner air and water, and safer automobiles, all of which was part of a massive attempt to make America a healthier and more equitable society. Johnson's forceful personality and powerful political skills moved the Great Society legislation through Congress over the strong objections of a group of southern Democrats and Republicans, including the staunch Republican senator from Arizona, Barry Goldwater.

While LBJ guided the Democrats and the nation in a liberal direction, Goldwater became the spiritual leader of a conservative swing among Republicans. Goldwater spoke for a growing body of conservative Americans who opposed the expanding role of the federal government into areas such as welfare, medical care, education, and civil rights, while favoring an end to diplomatic relations with all communist nations.

A genuine "Draft Goldwater" movement made the Arizona senator a reluctant presidential candidate in early 1963, over the serious opposition of the moderate wing of the party. As the badly divided Republicans approached the convention in July 1964, Nixon saw two ways in which he might again become involved in political life. Should the convention reach a deadlock, he would be in the wings as a compromise presidential candidate. Should Goldwater arrive at the convention the certain nominee, then Nixon could assume the role of party healer and try to reunite the factions that had been driven so far apart by the nomination process. Either way, there was a role for Nixon.

The convention belonged to Goldwater and the conservatives. Once convinced of that, Nixon introduced Goldwater to the convention with a speech that urged the party faithful to forget past differences and rally behind the candidate to ensure a Republican victory. Goldwater accepted the nomination and ran on a platform that called for curbing the powers of the federal government at home and the communists abroad.

UPI/BETTMANN NEWSPHOTOS

The widowed Jacqueline Kennedy at the funeral of President Kennedy, who was assassinated in 1963. Kennedy's death was the beginning of Nixon's reemergence in national politics.

National Guardsmen in Detroit, where there were riots in predominantly black areas in July 1967. Despite the civil rights legislation enacted as part of Johnson's Great Society programs, racial tension increased in the late 1960s as blacks grew impatient with the slow pace of economic and social progress.

Johnson became the Democratic nominee. He had no serious opposition. The Democratic platform endorsed the promises of the Great Society — to eliminate unemployment and poverty and make equal opportunity available to all Americans.

The presidential campaign of 1964 exaggerated the differences between the liberal and conservative sides of the American political system. Johnson was portrayed as a dangerous ultraliberal who was pushing the United States toward state socialism. Goldwater's casual remarks about the use of atomic weapons made people nervous; they worried that if he became president, he would destroy the world in a moment of nuclear madness. The campaign was described as "vicious and bitter."

Nixon, as always, was the hardworking party trooper. After trying to unite the party at the convention, he campaigned actively throughout the fall. Nixon knew that Goldwater could not win, yet he traveled 50,000 miles in 36 states during the six weeks before the election — more campaigning than

Goldwater did. In later years, party loyalists remembered Nixon's service to the party and to Republican candidates running for lesser offices during the bleak months of the 1964 election.

Goldwater suffered one of the worst defeats of any presidential candidate in American history. The voters emphatically rejected the conservative movement that he led, leaving the Republicans deeply divided. The split between the conservatives and the rest of the party seemed irreconcilable.

One Republican came out of the rubble of Goldwater's defeat in good shape. By carefully remaining neutral during the nominating process, Nixon had avoided being identified with one Republican faction against another. His active campaigning for Goldwater and other Republican candidates earned him high marks for party loyalty. After the Republican humiliation of 1964, Nixon looked toward the resurrection of the party and his own career. He believed both could be accomplished by his continued service to the party.

> *He is the least authentic man alive. . . . There is one Nixon only, though there seem to be new ones all the time — he will try to be what people want.*
> —GARRY WILLS
> journalist and historian

The off-year elections of 1966 gave him an opportunity to test his plan. Nixon sought no political office, but he campaigned everywhere. He appeared in 35 states on behalf of 86 Republican candidates. As a national figure, his presence brought a lot of media and voter attention to Republicans seeking office, and it was estimated that he helped raise $4 to $5 million for those candidates. The hundreds of speeches and the millions of dollars were the tools Nixon used to rebuild the party and his career. The Republicans gained 47 House seats, 3 Senate seats, and 6 governorships, successes for which Nixon deserves a generous share of the credit.

His role as a neutral party healer in 1964 won him the support of Goldwater conservatives. His contributions to Republican candidates in 1964 and again in 1966 earned him the debt of the young, pragmatic Republicans who were gaining control of the party. By 1967 both groups viewed Nixon as the real leader of the Republican party and the natural presidential nominee in 1968. A poll showed that rank and file Republicans supported that judgment.

Nixon moved cautiously until early 1968. Then he started expanding his staff and making his move. After the early primary elections in the spring, he emerged as the most serious Republican candidate, winning some states with over 70 percent of the votes cast. Nixon got his second chance at the presidency.

The Democrats made it easy for Nixon. Johnson had pushed forward his Great Society after the decisive victory over Goldwater in 1964, but he had also expanded America's role in the war in Vietnam, in which the United States was supporting the South Vietnamese government against the communist regime in North Vietnam and insurgents within South Vietnam, known as the Viet Cong. While a majority of Americans supported the lofty goals of Johnson's federal programs, opposition to the war in Vietnam grew as American involvement there increased. The war's opponents insisted that the United States was intervening in what was essentially an internal dispute that should be left to the Vietnamese themselves to decide. America was

fighting a limited war with no defined objectives, critics argued, and was risking a protracted and increasingly costly involvement with no concrete benefits to be realized and no chance of winning. Furthermore, the nature of the war — a guerrilla conflict that almost by definition invloved large segments of the civilian population — and Johnson's policy, announced in February 1965, of sustained bombing of North Vietnam, including civilian targets, made the American presence immoral and inhumane. Johnson had promised during his 1964 campaign not to send American boys to fight an Asian war, but by the end of 1965 there were 185,000 Americans in Vietnam and by 1967 the number had swelled to 400,000.

The North Vietnamese city of Haiphong after a U.S. bombing raid in January 1968. By the time Nixon was inaugurated, more bombing tonnage had fallen on Vietnam than on all of Europe during World War II.

The nation used the terms "hawks" and "doves" to identify supporters or opponents of the war. There was widespread opposition to the draft of young men to serve as soldiers. Demonstrations at induction centers and on college campuses became commonplace. In October 1967 a gathering of antiwar groups met in Washington, and U.S. marshals and military units were required to protect the Pentagon. Racial violence also increased. Riots broke out in ghettos in Detroit, Newark, and other American cities in 1967, followed by even more violence in more cities in the wake of the April 4, 1968, assassination of black civil rights leader Martin Luther King, Jr.

An enraged student at the University of Wisconsin speaks for millions of Americans in condemning the Vietnam War. As a presidential candidate in 1968 Nixon claimed to have a secret plan for ending the war, but the continued U.S. presence there further divided the country.

Violence, racism, and the war in Vietnam divided the nation and the Democratic party. Johnson responded to criticism of his Vietnam policy by sending more troops to try to win the war.

The increased costs of the war, coupled with the tremendous costs of the Great Society's social programs, threatened the domestic economy, causing inflation and rising taxes. The social programs of Johnson's Great Society felt the pinch. Traditional supporters within the Democratic party — intellectuals, blacks, liberals, organized labor — who had remained loyal to Johnson because of their faith in his social programs, now started to oppose the president, convinced that the Great Society would become a victim of the Vietnam war. They were correct.

President Johnson escalated the Vietnam War while trying to enact the comprehensive social reform programs known as the Great Society. His surprising withdrawal from the presidential race in 1968 marked the failure of his Vietnam policy.

Organized opposition within the Democratic party to Johnson's renomination began to form a year before the election. In November 1967 Senator Eugene McCarthy of Minnesota announced that he would seek the Democratic nomination. The nation's first presidential primary in 1968 was held in New Hampshire. Running as an antiwar candidate, McCarthy polled an extremely strong 42 percent of the Democratic votes cast, to 48 percent for the incumbent president. McCarthy's showing was considered a moral victory and indicated the strength of the opposition to Johnson's Vietnam policy. Encouraged by McCarthy's success, Senator Robert Kennedy of New York, brother of the assassinated president, announced that he too would seek the nomination, also as an antiwar candidate, bringing the magic of the Kennedy name and the large following it commanded into the race. Antiwar groups and disenchanted Democrats rallied behind the new candidates.

In Vietnam the war was going badly for the Amer-

In his presidential campaign of 1968, Nixon tried to present a new image, but his greatest asset was the reluctance of his opponent, Hubert Humphrey, to disassociate himself from Johnson's Vietnam policy.

ican forces. Early in the year televised news coverage of the Tet offensive (*Tet* is the Vietnamese new year) by the North Vietnamese and the Viet Cong seemed to put the lie to Johnson's assertions that the war was winnable and under control, as nightly news programs showed footage of the communist forces attacking several key South Vietnamese cities. Americans at home watched as the communists overran the ancient provincial capital of Hue, surrounded an American garrison at Khe Sanh, and even threatened the U.S. Embassy in Saigon.

His poor showing in the New Hampshire primary made Johnson's lack of support clear, and it was evident that his candidacy would further polarize an already divided nation. On March 31, with an anticipated defeat in the Wisconsin primary of April 2 looming, Johnson used the opportunity of a televised speech in which he also announced a halt to much of the bombing of North Vietnam to say that he would not run for reelection. The war in Vietnam had defeated him.

Antiwar demonstrators clash with police at the 1968 Democratic National Convention in Chicago, in what was termed a "police riot." The city's mayor, Richard Daley, ordered the police to "shoot to kill" rioters.

Johnson's vice-president, Hubert H. Humphrey, a former senator with good liberal credentials, announced he would seek the nomination. Humphrey received Johnson's endorsement in return for agreeing to continue Johnson's policies in Vietnam.

Nineteen-sixty-eight was a turbulent year. Civil rights and antiwar demonstrations became more frequent and more violent. The cities exploded following the assassination of Martin Luther King, Jr. On the night of June 4, while Robert Kennedy celebrated his victory in the California primary, he was shot and killed by an assassin. Two months later, when the Democratic convention met in Chicago, police and antiwar demonstrators clashed in bloody skirmishes that filled television screens across the nation. In what was later officially described as a "police riot," the Chicago police beat and clubbed nearly everyone within their reach — men and women, demonstrators and innocent bystanders, convention delegates and reporters.

Inside the Chicago International Amphitheater the antiwar forces and the Humphrey forces carried out their own battle, but they all knew who the nominee would be. While McCarthy and Kennedy had battled for control of the antiwar vote in the primaries, Humphrey had cornered the support of enough professional politicians and delegates to win the nomination. He chose Senator Edmund S. Muskie of Maine as his vice-president. The platform supported the programs and policies of the Johnson years, including the Vietnam War. Humphrey won the nomination with Johnson's support; he would lose the election with Johnson's war.

The Republicans selected their nominee in Miami Beach. Nixon put together a smooth-running and experienced campaign staff that functioned well in the primaries and then moved swiftly to control the convention. By the time he arrived in Miami, Nixon was assured of the necessary votes, which he received on the first ballot. The surprise of the convention was Nixon's selection of the relatively unknown governor of Maryland, Spiro Agnew, as his running mate.

Nixon and the Republican platform checked off the nation's ills and laid them at the Democrat's doorstep — crime in the streets, cities in crisis, racial tensions, poverty, unemployment, and the war in Vietnam.

Nixon's admirers said he was ready for the presidency. There was much talk about the "New Nixon." Supporters claimed that his time out of office had been good for him. He seemed more relaxed and more personable, less intense and combative. His acceptance speech at the convention and his general style and tone during much of the campaign supported the idea of a "New Nixon." Given the passion and anger that surrounded so many of the issues of 1968, Nixon appeared restrained.

His campaign was designed to cultivate the "New Nixon" image, to convince voters that he was no longer the same person who had won elections with unattractive and unethical tactics, such as those he used in the Voorhis and Douglas elections. He abandoned the exhausting whistle-stop methods of 1960

Let us begin by committing ourselves to the truth — to see it like it is, and tell it like it is — to find the truth, to speak the truth, and to live the truth.
—RICHARD NIXON
accepting the Republican presidential nomination, 1968

Having hoped for a broad mandate in the 1968 election, Nixon was unhappy with his margin of victory. Although he won a clear majority of the electoral votes, the popular vote (total number of ballots cast) was extremely close.

and 1962, which gave the public and the press uncontrolled access to him, in favor of well-orchestrated media events, many of which were taped at hand-picked gatherings and were designed to show the candidate to best advantage on the evening news programs. Nixon's strategists kept him away from crowds, reporters, and events that they could not control; they were so careful and fearful about the press that it became almost impossible for any reporters except the most friendly to interview him. Public and spontaneous access to Nixon was eliminated and was replaced by a brilliant use of radio and television, perhaps the best media campaign seen so far. As it turned out, only the way Nixon was presented to the public was new.

Nixon attacked Humphrey for being part of the administration that was responsible for the nation's troubles, but he avoided the old-style character assaults. He hammered on the issues — law and order (a catchphrase for disapproval of antiwar and black-power demonstrations), inflation, federal spending, truth in government, the rising crime rate, deterioration of the inner cities, and Vietnam. Nixon was cautious on the war issue, which had already defeated Johnson. He insisted he had a secret plan that would end the war but could not go public with it for fear it would jeopardize peace talks then taking place in Paris, France. Many voters saw Nixon as the man who would end America's involvement in Vietnam and Humphrey as the candidate who would continue it. American war dead already numbered over 32,000.

When the votes were counted in November, Nixon was the 37th president of the United States. Humphrey's campaign caught fire at the end after he took several steps to disassociate himself from Johnson's Vietnam policy, and so Nixon was denied the landslide many had predicted for him. Nixon did not have the overwhelming mandate he wanted so badly, but he had the presidency.

The resurrection of Richard Nixon is one of the dramatic comeback stories in American political history. Defeated for the presidency and then for a governorship, a humbled Nixon was written off as a national politician, but the misfortune of others and his own political instincts enabled him to come back. Certainly the assassination of John Kennedy, the electoral humiliation of Barry Goldwater, the Vietnam failures of Lyndon Johnson, the assassination of Robert Kennedy, and the inability of Hubert Humphrey to separate himself from Johnson's war all worked to Nixon's advantage. But Nixon's return was not all attributable to luck. He was shrewd and hardworking enough to sit tight after the 1962 defeat, to remain neutral and thus be in a position to unify the Republican party in 1964, and to stump tirelessly for Republican candidates in 1964 and again in 1966. His discipline and instincts made him the party leader and certain nominee in 1968.

The "New Nixon" tactics played on the fact that much of the nation was weary of the tensions and divisiveness that arose from the issues of the 1960s. Although many of Americans believed in the programs of the Great Society, many also wanted a return to normal life in America. Nixon shrewdly addressed his campaign and his presidency to them, appealing to what he called a "silent majority" of Americans — those Americans whose voices were not heard at protests and demonstrations; who were fed up with domestic disturbances, disrespect for authority, and crime; who looked at welfare recipients and wondered what had happened to the work ethic; who remained proud of the country and the government yet were dissatisfied with the direction in which they saw the nation heading. The "New Nixon" portrayed himself as a conciliator who stood for basic virtues and a restored pride in America.

His inaugural address played on quiet themes. He asked Americans to lower their voices, to leave behind the "fever of words" and the "angry rhetoric" that divided the nation. He spoke about "the better angles of our nature," and about celebrating the "simple things — such as goodness, decency, love, kindness." He promised to "bring us together."

Despite his efforts to quiet them, the voices remained angry during Nixon's first term in office. Many concerned Americans traveled to Washington,

In July 1969 U.S. astronauts Neil Armstrong and Edwin Aldrin (pictured) became the first men to walk on the moon. Many Americans asked whether the money used for the space program would be more useful combating America's social and environmental problems.

The 1972 Democratic presidential and vice-presidential candidates, George Mc-Govern (center, right) and Thomas Eagleton (far left), with their 1968 counterparts, Humphrey (center, left) and Edmund Muskie (far right). The voters overwhelmingly rejected the Democratic ticket in 1972.

D.C., from near and far to demand an end to the war. Still, it dragged on. Thirteen thousand more American soldiers had died by early 1972, bringing the total to over 45,000, with no end in sight. Opposition to the war was not confined to the college campuses in California and the East Coast; it became commonplace in every corner of the land, dividing friends, homes, and the nation.

Nixon faced reelection in 1972 with most of Johnson's problems now his. The national mood craved an end to the war and solutions for pressing domestic problems — drugs, violence, unemployment, segregated schools, racism, the unequal legal status

70

of women, and the need to protect the environment. Nixon, like Johnson, seemed impotent on those matters that most distressed the nation.

Defeating an incumbent president is always difficult, but the Democrats appeared hopeful as they geared up for the election of 1972. George McGovern, a candidate who spoke for the liberal wing of the party, emerged from the primary season as the frontrunner. The soft-spoken senator from South Dakota combined the moral tone of his religious upbringing, the intellectual content of his Ph.D. in history, and the urgency of the antiwar movement and forged them into a powerful force. He brought the voices of dissenting Americans into the political mainstream by promising to bring all American soldiers home from Vietnam and to solve America's domestic problems with funds taken from a reduced military budget.

His candidacy split the party. Many traditional Democratic groups, particularly party bosses and organized labor, were offended by McGovern's opposition to the war and his support for abortion, increased welfare, full employment, federal health insurance, and amnesty for Vietnam draft resisters. They decided to sit out the election, and by so doing, they ensured the reelection of Richard Nixon.

McGovern did enormous damage to his own candidacy during the Eagleton crisis. Soon after the convention, it became known that McGovern's vice-presidential nominee, Senator Thomas Eagleton of Missouri, had been hospitalized three times for emotional problems and had received electricshock therapy. McGovern's first response was a public statement backing Eagleton "1,000 percent," but he soon realized that keeping Eagleton on the ticket would doom his candidacy and asked for Eagleton's resignation. Eagleton complied and returned to the Senate, where he continued a distinguished career. In time McGovern became his own harshest critic of the way he handled the Eagleton crisis, but in the fall of 1972 it was the voters who saw McGovern as cold, calculating, and two-faced — epithets that in the past had often been used by his opponents to describe Nixon.

Nixon campaigned in 1972 from a position of strength, using his standing as incumbent president to advantage. His foreign policy successes in arranging summit meetings with the Soviet Union and China served him well in this regard.

While the Democratic campaign self-destructed, Nixon's situation improved steadily. Nixon skillfully used the power of the incumbent president to his best advantage. He planned to use the high office to its best advantage by remaining in the White House as long as possible during the campaign and gaining all the attention he could muster from his job as president. He shifted the nation's attention away from Vietnam and domestic problems and focused it on a series of spectacular foreign affairs initiatives — détente, a strategic arms limitation agreement with the Soviet Union, and summit meetings with the Soviet Union and China. The two summits in particular were highly successful, and the press attention was favorable.

His campaign strategy also called for extensive use of computerized direct mailings, telephone campaigns, and sophisticated surveys to influence and rally as many votes as possible for the president. The Nixon campaign team was again able to use the same type of carefully arranged television appearances that had worked so effectively during the 1968 campaign. The "New Nixon" was able to use the prestige of the White House and techniques of modern campaigning to maintain a safe distance between himself and the voters.

These strategies had a single goal — to earn Nixon an overwhelming reelection victory. They made no provisions for Republican candidates who were running for the House of Representatives, the Senate, and state houses — the very sort of party loyalty on which Nixon had rebuilt his career.

Nixon faced only token opposition to renomination. In a Miami convention that was notable because it ran on schedule, the confident Republicans nominated Nixon and Agnew. The national campaign was unusual in that the candidates differed openly and significantly on the many issues — Vietnam, domestic problems (school integration, amnesty for draft resisters, drugs, abortion, the environment), the proper balance between military and domestic spending.

Nixon was not able to resolve these issues or quiet the citizens who were distressed over them, but his experience in foreign affairs and his successful negotiations at summits in Moscow and Beijing (Peking) convinced voters that he was a decisive and effective leader. The image of the "New Nixon" and the White House strategy worked. Many traditional Democratic groups defected to Nixon — the South, blue-collar voters, the young, and Catholics in some parts of the country. Nixon got his second term and the overwhelming victory he wanted so badly, winning 60.69 percent of the popular vote and 49 states.

5

The Nixon Presidency: Foreign Affairs

Nixon had long considered foreign affairs an area of expertise. He considered his trips abroad as Eisenhower's representative among the most valuable experiences of his term as vice-president, and he arrived in the White House in 1968 having given careful consideration to the conduct of U.S. foreign policy.

The secretary of state has traditionally served the president as the cabinet officer responsible for the implementation of foreign policy, but Nixon believed that only the president should determine foreign policy. He also very strongly believed that the State Department was too bureaucratic to participate constructively in decision making and was likely to interfere with his new method of conducting foreign policy. So, Nixon appointed William Rogers, a man who admitted to having little foreign policy experience, as secretary of state. Rogers' responsibility was to make sure that the entrenched bureaucracy at Foggy Bottom, the State Department's headquarters, carried out Nixon's directives.

It is time that we started to act like a great nation around the world.
—RICHARD NIXON
1968

Nixon was determined to set his own foreign policy, unencumbered by the State Department or Congress. His penchant for secrecy and arrogation of government power to himself led critics to term his administration "the imperial presidency."

American B-52 bombers hit North Vietnamese artillery positions in 1967. Nixon ordered the resumption of the bombing of North Vietnam that Johnson had halted in 1968.

Nixon's appointee as head of the National Security Council, Henry Kissinger, a refugee from Nazi Germany and a celebrated professor of international politics at Harvard University, was to serve as his chief adviser in foreign affairs. The unlikely duo — the Jewish professor and the Quaker politician — reshaped America's foreign policy. Kissinger's negotiating skills and extraordinary intelligence, together with Nixon's willingness to exercise power and their common vision of world affairs, made foreign affairs the focus of Nixon's administration.

As he came to power in 1969, the war in Vietnam was the most difficult foreign-policy challenge Nixon faced. He set an "honorable end to the war in Vietnam" as his first priority.

Since the end of World War II, U.S. policy toward Vietnam had been shaped by one principle: preventing Vietnam from becoming a unified nation under a communist ruler. Nixon always claimed that self-determination for the South Vietnamese people, a government of their choice, was the goal of American involvement in the war. The U.S. supported a series of governments located in South Vietnam against the communists in the North. By the time Nixon took office, the United States had committed over 500,000 American troops and millions of dollars in aid to the war.

Nixon had been coy about Vietnam during the 1968 election. He claimed to have a secret plan for achieving "a peace we can live with and to be proud of." Once revealed, his plan to end the fighting consisted of bombing North Vietnam, tough negotiations, and gradual withdrawal of U.S. troops. Nixon's ideas for bringing peace to Vietnam were not new, but his emphasis was. Wanting a negotiated peace that would remove American forces from Vietnam and ensure an independent South Vietnam, he would concentrate his efforts on a diplomatic victory instead of a military one. He would use military might to reinforce his negotiating position. America's role as world leader was to be upheld, strengthened by an honorable end to an extremely unpopular war.

A massive antiwar demonstration along Pennsylvania Avenue in Washington, D.C., in 1971 demonstrates the hostility that Nixon's Vietnam policy aroused. Nixon's expansion of the war into Cambodia and Laos increased domestic opposition to the war.

UPI/BETTMANN NEWSPHOTOS

Nixon's policy of Vietnamization proposed the gradual withdrawal of U.S. troops while South Vietnamese soldiers were trained to take their place. After the U.S. withdrawal in April 1973 the South Vietnamese army suffered repeated defeats, ultimately surrendering to the North Vietnamese in April 1975.

Peace eluded Nixon. As the war dragged on, and the toll of American dead grew, Johnson's war became Nixon's war. To inherit the war was to inherit the antiwar movement. By late 1969 a poll showed that a majority of Americans believed involvement in Vietnam was a mistake. As antiwar sentiment grew, antiwar demonstrations grew larger and more frequent.

In the fall of 1969 Nixon began a program to undercut his critics. He counterattacked the demonstrators, whom he described as "bums," and he rallied the silent majority, who largely agreed with his conduct of the war. Then he instructed Vice-president Spiro Agnew to undertake a campaign designed to intimidate critics of his Vietnam policy. Presidents of television networks were called with complaints about the evening news, and newspaper editors were asked to rein in their White House reporters and tone down critical reports. Agnew gave a series of inflammatory speeches in which he attacked Nixon's critics as ignorant, unpatriotic fools who were aiding the communists, betraying freedom, and destroying America. His outrageous characterizations alarmed many fair-minded Americans. Nixon, Agnew, and the people around them insisted that their critics were actually dedicated enemies, that dissenters were really communist dupes, and that the news media was part of a liberal conspiracy that was dedicated to destroying the Nixon presidency.

Nixon also unveiled "Vietnamization" as part of his plan for ending the war. As Nixon described it in the fall of 1969, American troops would be gradually phased out of the fighting and sent home as the South Vietnamese army received the necessary training and equipment to defend their country. It was an old idea that had succeeded and failed cyclically in the past, but Nixon was committed to it. He announced that 60,000 of the 540,000 American soldiers in Vietnam would soon be on their way home.

By the spring of 1970 it appeared as though Nixon had control of the Vietnam situation. He explained over national TV that Vietnamization was going so well that another 150,000 men would soon be withdrawn. The reduction in troops, Agnew's attack on critics of the war, and major revisions in the draft laws (that made the draft fairer) took much of the energy out of the antiwar movement. Both the war and opposition to it appeared to be winding down.

However, Nixon then ordered the invasion of Cambodia, in the late spring of 1970, and Laos, in February 1971. Both were neighboring countries of Vietnam that had struggled to remain neutral in the fighting. Nixon claimed that "Communist aggression" in those countries threatened the Vietnamization program and made the invasions necessary. The U.S. action was also intended to strike at the so-called Ho Chi Minh trail, which ran through the mountainous region of Laos along the South Vietnamese border and was used by the Viet Cong and North Vietnamese to transport men and matériel. The invasion of Cambodia was also intended to support the government of Lon Nol, recently installed in a U.S.-supported coup, against domestic communist opposition, the Khmer Rouge.

The Vietnam War was essentially a guerilla war in which the enemy was often unseen and indistinguishable from the civilian population. The lack of clear military objectives and the war's unpopularity undermined the military's morale.

He failed to say that he had earlier authorized bombings and military operations in Cambodia but had kept them secret from the American people. The world was shocked and stunned when America invaded two neutral nations to pursue peace in Vietnam.

Neither invasion produced the military results that Nixon hoped for. Thousands of civilians were killed, and the war that most Americans wanted ended grew larger. Nixon's policy was particularly disastrous for Cambodia, where the destabilization that followed in the wake of the installation of Lon Nol and the U.S. bombing and invasion helped contribute to a bloody civil war and the ultimate victory of the Khmer Rouge, whose brutal regime was responsible for the death of between 700,000 and 2 million Cambodian people. The South Vietnamese army was badly bloodied in Laos. As the beaten South Vietnamese troops fled back across the border, it was a vivid reminder that the fate of that army was also the fate of Nixon's Vietnamization program. Both were in shambles.

On May 4, 1970, National Guardsmen fired into a crowd of students attending Kent State University in Kent, Ohio. The students were protesting Nixon's decision to send U.S. troops into Cambodia. Four students were killed and eleven others wounded.

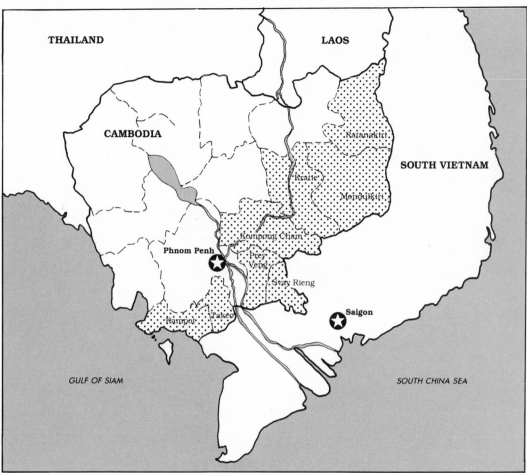

THAILAND

LAOS

CAMBODIA

SOUTH VIETNAM

Ratanakiri

Kratie

Mondulkiri

Kompong Cham

Phnom Penh

Prey Veng

Svay Rieng

Saigon

Kampot

Takeo

GULF OF SIAM

SOUTH CHINA SEA

The invasions of Cambodia and Laos signaled the failure of Nixon's Vietnam policy. The antiwar movement had gained new momentum in early 1970 with the revelation that an American force under Lieutenant William Calley had massacred Vietnamese civilians, including women and children, at the hamlet of My Lai. News of the invasions sparked further dissent. Campuses across the country erupted. At Kent State University and Jackson State College innocent students were shot and killed by National Guardsmen and police in the spring of 1970. Washington, D.C., saw one of the worst riots in its history in April 1971. Antiwar critics gained fresh converts. Average Americans who had long supported Nixon's conduct of the war became angry when their president lied to them about Cambodia.

The shaded areas represent Cambodian regions controlled by North Vietnamese and Viet Cong troops in 1970. They were sometimes referred to as sanctuaries because they were used as staging grounds for communist raids into South Vietnam and could not be attacked because Cambodia was officially a neutral country.

81

UPI/BETTMANN NEWSPHOTOS

A Cambodian boy displays his peace sign medallion to American troops. The U.S. invasion was disastrous for Cambodia. Bombing ravaged the countryside, and the civil war that followed was won by the communist Khmer Rouge, who were notorious for their brutality.

I'm not going to be the first American president who loses a war.

—RICHARD NIXON
on Vietnam

In the summer of 1971 *The New York Times* began publication of the *Pentagon Papers*, an account of military decision making in Vietnam based on confidential Defense Department documents and leaked by a former Pentagon official, Daniel Ellsberg. The *Papers* showed that Kennedy and Johnson had long misled the public about their intentions in Vietnam. Nixon obtained an injunction to stop publication, but the Supreme Court overturned the order. It was at this time that Nixon first approved the creation of the "White House Plumbers," who were charged with plugging leaks within the government and discrediting Ellsberg.

The invasion of Cambodia and Laos and the revelations of My Lai and the *Pentagon Papers* seemed to give many Americans a new insight into the nature of the war being fought in Vietnam. Weary of an expanded war that seemed to have no end, they were appalled at the death and destruction being ordered by their government. Napalm, bombing, and ground fighting destroyed villages and farms, cost 1.2 million Vietnamese lives, and ravaged a country that the war was intended to preserve. Americans wanted Nixon to end the fighting, stop the suffering, and bring the troops home.

82

Nixon, like Johnson before him, did not want to be remembered in history as the first American president to lose a war. He pushed on with his three-part plan. He turned to the air war in early 1972. In April he ordered the bombing of North Vietnam for the first time since 1968. Massive waves of B-52s swept over the cities of Hanoi and Haiphong. The next month he mined North Vietnam's internal waterways and major ports to keep out ships carrying military supplies, a dangerous move, charged critics, who warned that a Russian or Chinese ship might be sunk.

In the summer and fall of 1972 attention turned to Paris and the peace talks. Begun during Johnson's presidency, over 150 meetings had produced no results. But secret meetings between Kissinger and Le Duc Tho of North Vietnam, long rumored, brought Kissinger's October announcement that "peace is at hand." Kissinger's private negotiations with the North Vietnamese had at long last brought terms both parties found acceptable, but the South Vietnamese government reversed their earlier position and objected to the agreement. Talks were set to resume in a few weeks.

UPI/BETTMANN NEWSPHOTOS

Nixon's chief foreign affairs adviser, Henry Kissinger (right), and North Vietnam's Le Duc Tho negotiated a settlement to the Vietnam War in January 1973. Their efforts earned them the Nobel Peace Prize, but the peace was short-lived.

In 1972 Nixon became the first U.S. president to visit China, resuming official government relations between the two nations, which had been broken off after the Chinese revolution in 1949. Here, Nixon visits the Great Wall of China.

The North Vietnamese resisted the new South Vietnamese terms and even reneged on some terms they had agreed to in October. Kissinger persisted and managed to get North Vietnamese agreement on the October text. The talks broke off on December 13 with only the status of a demilitarized zone in question. The next day Nixon retaliated by ordering American planes back into the air over North Vietnam's cities. The B-52s had military and industrial targets, but they hit homes, schools, and hospitals as well. Two weeks of around-the-clock bombing devastated parts of North Vietnam (nearly 3,000 civilians were killed in Hanoi alone during raids on Christmas Eve) and brought the North Vietnamese back to Paris to talk about peace.

On January 27, 1973, the parties signed a treaty to end the war. Nixon announced "peace with honor," but its terms were not to last. There was little honor for returning servicemen. They were greeted not with parades and marching bands as in the past but with silence and shame. America's reputation abroad was tarnished as well. The main provisions were the same as those Nixon had fought against prior to the deadly December bombings. The treaty stopped the fighting but designated a demilitarized zone between North and South Vietnam that was "provisional and not a political and territorial boundary." This language all but ensured the unification of North and South Vietnam into one country — the critical issue America had fought to prevent for so long, with so many lives. The release of American prisoners of war — whose numbers increased when 15 B-52s were shot down during the December raids — was part of the bargain; in exchange, America agreed to have its few remaining troops out of the country in 60 days.

Nixon ended America's longest war. The human costs were staggering: 1.2 million dead Vietnamese, 58,000 dead Americans, 300,000 wounded Americans, 70,000 draft resisters. The psychological costs are beyond measure. The war in Vietnam divided America as nothing else had since the Civil War. Nixon is credited with ending the war, but in truth he only de-Americanized it. The war continued until

1975, when the North Vietnamese gained control of the South and unified the country. Nearly 45 percent of the Americans killed in Vietnam died during Nixon's years in office. The man who campaigned for the presidency in 1968 with a secret plan to end the war directed the fighting for four more years at a cost of 26,000 American lives.

Nixon did not confine his foreign policy initiatives to the seemingly endless process of bringing peace to Vietnam, but his two major successes — summits with China and the Soviet Union — were closely tied to that objective. He hoped that closer relations with the Soviet Union and China would aid the United States in its negotiations with Vietnam. Nixon believed that both countries would give him a free hand in dealing with North Vietnam in order to obtain closer relations with the United States.

While Nixon fought a war against the communists of North Vietnam, other aspects of his foreign policy reflected a changed attitude toward communism. During the 1950s and early 1960s, Nixon, like many Americans, believed in the theory of monolithic communism, the idea that all communist nations act in unison, largely taking their cue from the Soviet Union, even if to do so hurt their best interests as independent nations. As the leader of the communist bloc and the strongest of the communist nations, the Soviet Union was considered the biggest threat to the United States and the free world.

By 1968 Nixon, like many Americans, had a more realistic understanding of world politics. He no longer believed that the international arena should be viewed as a struggle for survival against the communists, as it had been since World War II. In his first inaugural address he announced that he wanted to end the feelings of "confrontation" between nations and replace it with "peaceful competition" and an "era of negotiations."

Nixon's more sophisticated worldview derived from Kissinger's theories of international politics. Instead of seeing just two competing powers — America and the Soviet Union — Kissinger saw many centers of power, including the United States, the Soviet Union, China, Japan, and the Western Eu-

Nixon returned from his China trip impressed by the pride of the Chinese in their culture and heritage and their dedication to improving their nation. Scientific and cultural exchanges between China and the U.S. soon followed.

ropean bloc. According to the Nixon Doctrine, as it became known, a successful foreign policy required a flexible and graceful management of America's relationship with all the powers so that each balanced the other, rather than competing against only one of them.

Nixon recognized that it would be nearly impossible to make his foreign policy work unless he normalized diplomatic relations with China. China had been an American ally during World War II, and friendly relations continued until 1949, when a communist government came to power. America, then struggling with its cold war fears, broke diplomatic relations and used its influence to keep China out of the United Nations. It was as though the world's most populous nation did not exist in the eyes of the United States.

With his new global view of foreign policy, Nixon sought to change that. He sent Kissinger to China, where the professor conducted a series of secret meetings over a period of nearly three years in preparation for a tour by Nixon. In the winter of 1972 Nixon became the first U.S. president to visit China. The trip was undertaken with one eye on the 1972 reelection campaign. Accompanied by a planeload of reporters and television crews, Nixon was photographed and filmed with Mao Zedong, the leader of China since the revolution of 1949, at a series of state meetings and spectacular events at such historic sites as the Great Wall of China. It was one of the best-staged summit meetings ever held. The entire world watched.

The two leaders concluded useful agreements. They agreed to cultural and scientific exchanges, to open trade, and soon thereafter to set up liaison offices in each country. By 1973 relations between the two countries were nearly normal. The summit eased over 20 years of hostility and antagonism between China and the United States and is considered a major diplomatic and public relations triumph for President Nixon. The China visit was the high point of Nixon's presidency and his years of public service.

Nixon hoped that his visit to China would have a

positive influence on relations between the United States and the Soviet Union as well. He wanted to play one country against the other. Nixon knew that the Soviets considered China a dangerous neighbor with whom it shared a 2,000-mile border. He correctly believed that the Soviet Union would seek friendlier ties with the United States in order to head off an alliance between its two chief rivals — the United States and China.

The China trip paved the way for a Nixon summit with Soviet leader Leonid Brezhnev in May 1972. As with the China visit, the Moscow summit was preceded by discreet and difficult negotiations conducted by Henry Kissinger. That summit was also a well-publicized event. The time was right for the two leaders to meet and talk. Because of the massive expenditure it entailed, both countries needed to slow the arms race that was a fixture of cold war politics. In addition to curbing the new Chinese-American friendship, the Soviet Union also wanted U.S. assistance in high technology and agriculture. Nixon sought to limit nuclear armaments, to increase trade, and to gain Soviet assistance in ending the Vietnam War.

In May 1972 Nixon visited the Soviet Union, where he and Soviet leader Leonid Brezhnev (seated at right) signed a nuclear arms limitation agreement (SALT I) aimed at ending the arms race between the two superpowers.

Brezhnev and Nixon toast the signing of SALT I. Nixon was struck by Brezhnev's expansive personality. He found the Soviet leader to be blunt, cordial, and shrewd and was impressed by his political ability and toughness.

Nixon and Brezhnev signed major arms limitation agreements during the Moscow summit. The SALT I (for "strategic arms limitations talks") agreements were cheered by the world as a symbolic gesture toward controlling the nuclear arms race and establishing a friendlier relationship between the two superpowers. Additional agreements on technology, sales of U.S. wheat, and future trade indicated that détente (a relaxation of tension between nations; often used by Kissinger to refer specifically to U.S.-Soviet relations) was in the offing.

The Moscow summit was a foreign-affairs success. The president signed the world's first nuclear arms limitation agreement. With cocktail in hand and an arm around Communist party chief Brezhnev, Nixon smiled for the cameras as the world's two most powerful leaders celebrated "peaceful coexistence" with 1,500 guests at the Kremlin.

Nixon's foreign policy and his diplomatic initiatives with China and the Soviet Union had some effect on the Vietnam negotiations. Nixon encircled North Vietnam diplomatically. As he had hoped, both the Soviet Union and China became more tolerant of U.S. actions in Vietnam because they did not want to jeopardize improved relations with the United States. This gave Nixon flexibility to act. For example, on the very eve of the Moscow summit,

Nixon mined the harbors of North Vietnam, thereby cutting off arms shipments from the Soviets. The Soviets chose to react mildly to that action rather than jeopardize the summit.

Nixon gambled correctly that East-West relations were more important to both China and the Soviet Union than their support for North Vietnam, but he overestimated the amount of influence that either country had on Vietnam, which took supplies from its communist allies but remained suspicious of them. The two nations might give Nixon the room he needed to maneuver the United States out of the war, but they lacked sufficient influence to force North Vietnam into peace terms it did not want.

When Nixon took office in 1968 he set his highest goals in foreign affairs, seeking nothing less than to reverse the national state of mind and course of action that had governed America's relations with the communist nations since World War II. With Henry Kissinger he worked to end the era of nuclear confrontation and to eliminate some of the mutual mistrust that characterized relations between the superpowers.

Nixon's foreign policy record is mixed. Nixon ended the war in Vietnam but only after four years in office and at a cost of thousands of American and Vietnamese lives. From the earliest days, critics of American involvement had argued that the South Vietnamese government could never survive alone, that the war could never be won, and that it was inevitable for Vietnam to become a united country under the control of the North. Yet Nixon, like other policymakers before him, continued a flawed policy in Vietnam long after most Americans and nearly all the leaders of friendly nations thought it a tragic mistake doomed to failure.

To the credit of the Nixon presidency, Nixon and Kissinger brought China into the world community by initiating discussions that led to full diplomatic relations between the two countries and admission to the United Nations. Nixon's Soviet summit produced a series of modest agreements and a symbolic arms limitation agreement, all of which contributed to a temporary thaw in American-Soviet relations.

The press is the enemy.
—RICHARD NIXON

6

Policy at Home

Although Vietnam and foreign affairs demanded a great deal of the president's time and energy, Nixon also had a domestic agenda. Speaking under the banner "New Federalism," Nixon promised to stop the flow of power and resources from the states into Washington and promised the return of "law and order"; wrapped inside both of those promises was the implication that he would undo many of the programs of Johnson's Great Society.

When he spoke about restoring "law and order," Nixon meant being tough on antiwar demonstrators, civil rights advocates, and certain types of criminals. Nixon believed that the Constitution and the courts were too protective of individual rights, such as the right to public demonstration and free speech. In an attempt to change that, he asked Congress to enact a "law and order" package of federal legislation (which would restrict some of those traditional American rights), and he tried to influence the courts in a more conservative direction.

> *I'm an introvert in an extrovert's profession.*
> —RICHARD NIXON

Senator Joseph Montoya questions a witness involved in the Watergate affair about the tapes of Nixon's White House conversations. The tapes provided incontrovertible evidence of the president's involvement in the cover-up of the Watergate burglary.

During his second visit to the Soviet Union, in 1974, Nixon and Brezhnev met at the Black Sea city of Yalta. Nixon was pleased that Brezhnev demonstrated continued interest in détente, but the meeting was overshadowed by the Watergate scandal.

Nixon hoped to change the Supreme Court by appointing conservative justices. He believed that under Chief Justice Earl Warren (ironically, an Eisenhower appointee) the court had gone too far in extending civil liberties (particularly to accused criminals) and civil rights and wanted tougher decisions that would restrict both. A more conservative court that acted in that fashion would help restore respect for authority throughout the country, he reasoned.

Nixon appointed a conservative chief justice, Warren Burger. When another vacancy came open, the Senate refused to confirm two Nixon nominees after both were charged with racist, incompetent, or unethical behavior. The sad truth is that by recommending men of such character and ability for the highest court in the land, Nixon hurt the reputation of the court and his quest to restore respect for authority. Nevertheless, before Nixon left office, his appointments shifted the court toward a conservative position, making possible some of the important decisions he wanted on criminals' rights, civil rights, and the death penalty.

Nixon proved to be even more conservative than his revised court when it came to civil rights for black Americans. As president, Nixon wanted to pull back from a governmentally enforced end to segregated school systems — one black, one white — even though they had been outlawed for 15 years. Nixon publicly denounced the idea of busing students in order to integrate schools. Never a champion of racial desegregation, Nixon argued that busing was not the best way to break down racial barriers, that the disruption it would cause in the schools would seriously impair education for all. He asked Congress to pass a law against busing, but neither Congress nor the courts — nor the American people — favored the continuation of segregated education. Over Nixon's objections, the courts pushed ahead with integration. By 1972 only 20 percent of southern blacks attended all-black schools, down from 80 percent in 1968. Many black leaders and civil rights advocates regard Nixon as the most antiblack president to sit in the White House in 50 years. Most historians agree.

In Moscow, passersby watch through the windows of a store as Nixon addresses the Russian people in a television broadcast during his 1974 visit. As impeachment proceedings continued to gather strength at home, many Americans still felt Nixon was performing well as president.

Senators Sam Ervin (top right) and Howard Baker (top left) headed the Senate committee investigating the Watergate affair. The televised hearings fascinated millions of Americans during the summer of 1973. Pictured on opposite page are former attorney general John Mitchell (top) and John Ehrlichman.

Although it appeared for a time as though Nixon had no real course of action for other domestic concerns, he eventually began dismantling Johnson's Great Society. He did not share the national goals of equal legal protection for minorities and women or the need for basic medical care, food, and shelter for all Americans. He reduced welfare benefits and spending for social-service agencies, including Job Corps and the National Institutes of Health, and he tried to do away with dozens of other programs concerned with urban renewal, hospital construction, school lunches, the unemployed, the mentally ill, veterans, and college students. In 1973 he abolished the Office of Economic Opportunity — the cornerstone of Johnson's War on Poverty.

At the same time he instituted revenue sharing, a program that returned many millions of tax dollars to state and local governments. Mayors and governors were pleased at first, until it became clear that they would become responsible for the people and programs that Nixon had eliminated.

Nixon inherited a troubled economy from Johnson. The Vietnam War and the Great Society were costly, and increased government spending caused inflation. When Nixon cut funding for domestic programs, he did so with the promise that those painful cuts would help curb inflation and balance the budget, but at the same time he reduced social programs, spending related to defense and the military increased, even after the war in Vietnam ended. Bigger expenditures kept inflation, unemployment, and consumer prices on an upward trend. The price of oil and gasoline tripled between 1973 and 1974 after the Organization of Petroleum Exporting Countries (OPEC) imposed an embargo on exports to the United States in protest of U.S. support for Israel in the Yom Kippur War against Egypt and Syria. Nixon failed to solve those economic problems, and they outlasted his presidency. The economy was his biggest domestic policy failure.

All other domestic events of Nixon's administration are overshadowed by Watergate. As a word, Watergate fails to convey the full meaning of the dark side of Richard Nixon's presidency. With the passage of time, it has come to encompass a long list of illegal and spiteful acts committed by the president and many of his advisers, associates, and advocates. The break-in at the Democratic National Committee headquarters was only a minor incident that spotlighted a host of criminal activities — misuse of federal agencies and funds, bribery, obstruction of justice, perjury, extortion, and a long list of campaign violations and infringements on civil liberties. Twenty-five Nixon aides and associates were guilty of Watergate-related crimes. Seventeen went to jail. Both the president and vice-president of the United States resigned from office. Considered in its entirety, Watergate is one of the most degrading stories in American political history.

The idea for the Watergate break-in surfaced at a meeting in the office of John Mitchell, the attorney general of the United States and Nixon's trusted friend and law partner from his New York days. Attorney General Mitchell discussed with members of the president's reelection committee an elaborate and expensive undertaking that involved kidnapping, prostitution, and electronic spying in order to gather information on the Democrats during the presidential election of 1972.

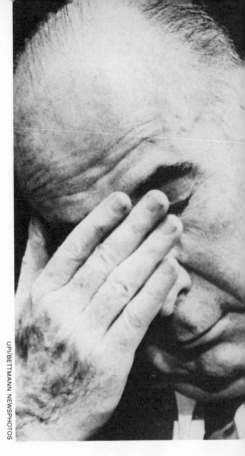

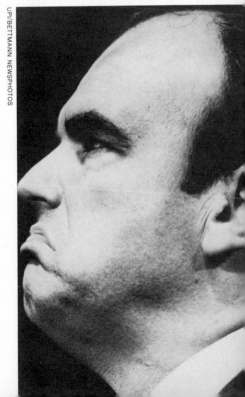

When Mitchell rejected the plan as too complicated and too expensive, the group settled on a scaled-down version; $89,000 in illegal campaign funds would finance a break-in at the headquarters of the Democratic National Committee in the Watergate complex.

The conspirators included former CIA agent E. Howard Hunt, a member of the White House staff and an author of spy novels, and a former FBI agent and lawyer for the reelection committee, G. Gordon Liddy, who would spend more time in jail than any other Watergate defendant.

The break-in took place on June 17, 1972. The police arrested five burglars (neither Hunt nor Liddy was there) and confiscated surveillance equipment and 32 $100 bills, all with consecutive numbers — not the sort of thing the average burglar carries on a job. The defendants gave no information to the police or the courts.

The cover-up began immediately, without hesitation. While Nixon's press secretary passed off the affair as a "third-rate burglary attempt," others in the White House were not so casual. Hunt's name turned up in one of the burglar's address books, and that worried insiders who knew Hunt had ties to the CIA as well as to the White House and that he and Liddy had engaged in other illegal activities on behalf of the Nixon administration. John Dean, the young, ambitious counsel to the president, and John Ehrlichman, the president's chief domestic adviser, conspired to destroy incriminating evidence in Hunt's White House office. The cover-up reached into the heart of the administration from the very beginning.

On June 23, less than a week after the break-in, Nixon became active in the conspiracy. He instructed his chief adviser, H. R. Haldeman, to order the CIA to block the FBI's investigation into the Watergate affair. He asked his personal attorney to take $75,000 from the reelection committee and see that it got into the hands of the Watergate defendants. The payment was the first of a grand total of $400,000. Later, when the defendants demanded more hush money, Nixon exploded, "For Christ

UPI/BETTMANN NEWSPHOTOS

G. Gordon Liddy, a counsel to the Committee to Reelect the President, was indicted for his role in planning the original Watergate burglary. He served more time in jail than any of the other Watergate defendants.

Judge John Sirica tried the original Watergate burglars. He was determined to find out the entire extent of the Watergate affair. The persistence of Sirica and the press eventually uncovered a series of criminal offenses and abuses of governmental power.

sake, get it!" He told everyone around him to "stonewall" it — deny everything, all involvement in a cover-up or prior knowledge of the break-in. He encouraged aides in the White House and at the reelection committee to lie under oath — to commit perjury — exactly as Alger Hiss had done before the HUAC committee. Hiss had gone to jail for perjury, just as Nixon's men would.

The cover-up held through the summer and fall of 1972. Nixon went on national TV to assure the American people that John Dean had conducted a thorough investigation that proved no cover-up existed. In reality no such investigation took place. In private, Nixon congratulated Dean for "putting your fingers in the dikes every time that leaks have sprung."

The break-in played a small part in the 1972 election. The press, particularly two young and relentless *Washington Post* reporters, Bob Woodward and Carl Bernstein, continued to gather bits and pieces of information and tried to fit the whole story together, but after Nixon's landslide the story seemed destined to die. Meanwhile, Judge John Sirica — known as "Maximum John" for his fondness for imposing harsh criminal sentences — was uneasy. He had presided over the trial of the Watergate defendants in early 1973. They all entered guilty pleas but refused to explain what they were doing at the Watergate. Convinced that there was more to the

Daniel Ellsberg leaked the *Pentagon Papers*, Defense Department documents that constituted a history of U.S. policy making in Vietnam, to *The New York Times*. The Nixon administration sought to prevent their publication.

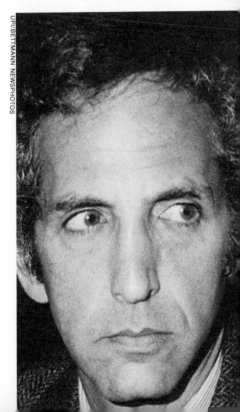

In October 1973 Vice-president Spiro T. Agnew resigned. Though Agnew's difficulties involved charges regarding his conduct while governor of Maryland and were unrelated to Watergate, his resignation reinforced the image of pervasive corruption throughout the Nixon administration.

story than a simple cover-up, Sirica pressured the defendants to speak up, threatening harsh sentences of up to 40 years in prison to encourage their cooperation. One of the defendants, James McCord, wrote Sirica a letter in which he alleged a massive cover-up. The story became front-page news once again.

A Senate investigating committee chaired by Senator Sam Ervin heard public testimony from a parade of witnesses in an attempt to unravel the details of Watergate. One after another Nixon's men appeared before the committee, took the oath, and denied everything, often with a smug arrogance that demeaned the proceedings. Meanwhile, Watergate grand jury prosecutors operated on the belief that several of Nixon's men from CREEP and the White House had lied under oath when they denied any knowledge of the affair. To catch them in perjury, and then promise them soft treatment on that charge, might encourage them to talk about Watergate.

Through the early months of 1973 more information surfaced while Nixon tried harder to maintain the cover-up. He would later claim that his efforts in the cover-up were attempts to contain the political damage Watergate was doing to the presidency and his abilities as chief executive, but too many people were pursuing the truth, and they were not about to stop short of the president of the United States to get it. The press, the courts, and the Senate produced a growing body of damning revelations. Nixon aides admitted that they committed perjury. They admitted to being involved in Watergate. Haldeman and Ehrlichman resigned and were indicted. Faced with such circumstances, Nixon agreed that there was a cover-up inside the White House but denied any personal knowledge of it. Yet Nixon's position was repeatedly undercut by a series of discoveries and revelations, the most dramatic of which came when John Dean, the White House counsel, testified before the Senate committee in the glare of TV cameras that the president had known about the cover-up early in its existence.

Additional revelations surfaced faster than the

White House could contradict them. Many were not connected to the break-in, but they demonstrated that illegal and unethical activities were commonplace in the Nixon administration. (Nixon maintained that his was not the first administration to use such tactics, that Kennedy and Johnson had been guilty of worse.) Dean explained that an "enemies list" of actors, entertainers, reporters, authors, clergy, and politicians whose chief offense was criticism of Richard Nixon was kept at the White House, thereby making them targets for harassment by the government — the FBI and the IRS were pressured to make life difficult for the "enemies." Related revelations showed that Nixon used federal agencies, particularly the FBI, to spy on domestic enemies such as those active in the antiwar movement. In their paranoia about leaks, the White House "plumbers" even tapped the phones of fellow staff members. Nixon's men arranged a burglary of Daniel Ellsberg's psychiatrist's office, hoping to obtain information that would discredit the man who had damaged the Nixon administration by releasing the *Pentagon Papers.*

> *When the president does it,*
> *that means it is not illegal.*
> —RICHARD NIXON

NATIONAL ARCHIVES

Nixon and Kissinger. Though Kissinger was linked to the wiretapping of White House staff members, he avoided much of the fallout from Watergate. He served as Ford's secretary of state after Nixon's resignation.

It was revealed that Nixon's closest friend, Bebe
Rebozo, mysteriously came into possession of
$100,000 in campaign funds that were never ac-
counted for. Of the millions of dollars in illegal
campaign contributions that financed Nixon's reelection in 1972, sizable sums came from corporate
contributors who expected—and got—the president
to use his influence on their behalf for illegal or
unethical purposes. Revelations about Nixon's personal finances caused the IRS to bill him for over
$450,000 in unpaid taxes. The president went on
national TV to assure an embarrassed nation, "I am
not a crook." In the middle of those revelations, Vice-
president Agnew, who had attracted so much attention by attacking Nixon's critics, resigned from
office after being indicted for bribery, extortion, tax
evasion, and conspiracy.

Finally, on March 1, 1974, the grand jury investigating the break-in and cover-up concluded its
work. Top Nixon aides and officials of his reelection
committee were indicted for conspiracy to obstruct
justice. Those indicted included John Mitchell,
Haldeman and Ehrlichman, and special counsel to
the president, Charles Colson. In a secret report,
the grand jury named Nixon a coconspirator but
chose not to indict him.

**Protesters demanded Nix-
on's impeachment at a rally
outside the White House in
October 1973. Nixon battled
the courts and Congress, determined to remain as president, but in August 1974 he
realized that the House of
Representatives was likely to
impeach him.**

WASHINGTON, D.C. PUBLIC LIBRARY

The fuel that propelled the Watergate scandals toward the president's resignation were revelations that Nixon had made tape recordings of conversations that took place in the White House Oval Office. They were a well-kept secret until July 1973, but from that point the Senate committee and the Watergate prosecutors fought to gain control of them. It was their belief that the tapes would confirm the substance of critical conversations that Dean spoke about before the Senate committee. If they did, then Nixon was surely guilty of obstruction of justice. For the year that followed, Nixon engaged in a bitter, last-ditch legal struggle to keep the tapes private.

On July 24, 1974, the Supreme Court ruled that Nixon had to release the tapes. The decision effectively ended his presidency. The tapes showed clearly a president who was part of the cover-up days after the break-in. The House Judiciary Committee recommended impeachment on July 27, 1974. Faced with certain conviction in the Senate, Nixon resigned from office the next week. The Nixon presidency was over.

Nixon was obviously under great stress during his emotional farewell speech to his staff. With him are his wife and daughter Tricia, who had made many speeches in defense of her father.

I impeached myself by resigning.
—RICHARD NIXON

7

The Politician

The stunning end of Richard Nixon's political career is a tale about the failure of a man and the nature of the American political system. Nixon's personal qualities and professional habits nourished the Watergate scandals. When he surrounded himself with people who lacked the ethical values required of good public servants, scandal became inevitable. The fault is not Nixon's alone. His rise to prominence was spectacularly swift. For whatever his failings, the Republican party and the nation rewarded him with public offices and gave him their approval until the very end.

Richard Nixon gave no signs of being burdened with a set of personal values or an ideology that slowed his ambition. His conversion into a professional anticommunist grew out of his baptism in the electoral process. The message was clear from the time of the Voorhis race in 1946 — anticommunism was worth votes. It did not matter whether your opponent was actually "soft on communism," so long as the charge garnered votes. It worked with Voorhis, with Helen Gahagan Douglas, with Alger Hiss, and it went a long way toward making Nixon the 39-year-old vice-president of the United States. The voters approved; so did the Republican party.

The often-told Watergate story is implicit, I think, in Nixon's whole career — the inability to trust others, even in his own government; the continued sense of grievance, even at the pinnacle of success; the overkill reaction to any challenge.
—GARRY WILLS
journalist and historian

Nixon leaves the White House for California after his farewell speech. In his inaugural address Ford expressed the hope that his predecessor, who had brought peace to millions, would find it for himself.

UPI/BETTMANN NEWSPHOTOS

The patterns of those early years stayed with Nixon; traces of them are found throughout Watergate. He did his best in situations where he could view opposing candidates not simply as adversaries in the give-and-take of the political arena but as dangerous antagonists whom he could attack without restraint. He was always on the prowl, looking for the critical element that could cast the other guy in the role of the villain. The "us or them" attitude became a central part of his style — Richard Nixon had no opponents, only enemies.

He was an unforgiving leader who longed for enough power to balance the ledger against critics and opponents, many of whom had done nothing more than publicly disagree with him. On the night of his election as president of the United States in 1968, while he watched the voter returns in the Pierre Hotel in New York, he discussed plans to use the authority of the presidency to make old enemies suffer. At the end of his presidency, at the time that Watergate was destroying his administration, he sat in the Oval Office and told an aide that he wanted "the most comprehensive notes on all those who have tried to do us in. They are asking for it and they are going to get it."

Nixon's rise to high office and his fall from power suggest a man who left his mark as a leader by feeding on the fears and anxiety of the voters while ignoring the finer side of the American spirit: assaulting the character of political opponents, implying people were Communists when he knew they were not, ordering Vice-president Agnew's vicious attack on his critics, compiling an "enemies list" while serving as president of the United States, praising a group of construction workers who beat up antiwar demonstrators, going on national TV and lying to the nation about the Cambodian invasion and Watergate, inflaming the nation over school integration. The list goes on. The White House tapes are filled with racial and ethnic slurs about "wops" and "Japs" as well as unkind references about friends, acquaintances, and supporters, many of whom were willing to go to jail for their president, and did.

Watergate seemed to confirm that Richard Nixon was everything his critics had charged all along. They insisted that he deserved the name "Tricky Dick" that they had given him years past. Political cartoonists, writers, and commentators ridiculed Nixon when they revived an old joke by asking all over again, "Would you buy a used car from this man?" For them, Watergate was the final affirmation of Nixon's worst qualities — secretiveness, manipulation, vindictiveness, and a lack of humanity and forgiveness — which demonstrated that after a lifetime in politics, he failed to understand the boundaries of the American political system.

Ronald Reagan (right) at a meeting of the HUAC in 1947. Nixon served as an unofficial foreign policy adviser to administration officials during the Reagan presidency.

UPI/BETTMANN NEWSPHOTOS

Nixon has always been concerned with his place in history, hoping that his presidency will be remembered for extricating the United States from Vietnam and for his foreign policy initiatives with the Soviet Union and China, rather than for the stigma of the Watergate affair and his resignation.

To judge Richard Nixon harshly as a politican and a leader is to invite other judgments as well. Nixon's youthful success as a politician could not have occurred without the approval of the voters and his party. The national climate of the late 1940s and the 1950s encouraged politicians to build their careers on anticommunism. California voters had three opportunities to reject Nixon and his campaign tactics before he ran for national office; they chose not to. The nation elected him president in 1968 and then reelected him by an overwhelming margin in 1972, even after the pattern of lies and deceptions was clear to many observers.

When Nixon ruined many lives as a leader of the McCarthy movement, he did so with the apparent support and approval of the majority. When he ran campaigns on half-truths and fabricated enemies that appealed to the prejudices of the people, he did so because the voters allowed him to. When Richard Nixon and the people in his administration broke laws and subverted the Constitution in an effort to defeat and punish their enemies, they did so after looking back over the president's long career and concluding that such behavior would be rewarded.

Richard Nixon's political career offers lessons in leadership and democracy that we ignore at great cost to the nation and our political system.

Almost one month to the day after assuming the office of president, former Vice-president Gerald R. Ford granted Richard Nixon "a full, free, and absolute pardon." Ford told the American public, "Our long national nightmare is over."

After his resignation Nixon lived a secluded life with his family on the San Clemente estate in California, working on his memoirs and other books and seeing few visitors. In 1976 he traveled to China, one of several trips where he was given a warm welcome and treated with the respect usually accorded a dignitary. He consented to a series of televised interviews with David Frost in 1977. *RN: The Memoirs of Richard Nixon* was published in 1978, *The Real War*, in 1980, *Leaders*, in 1982, and *Real Peace*, in 1984. In October 1981 he attended the funeral of Egyptian President Anwar Sadat, assassinated on the 8th anniversary of the Yom Kippur War. Included in the official American delegation, Nixon accompanied former presidents Jimmy Carter and Gerald Ford.

The Nixons moved to New York City in early 1980 and then to Saddle River, New Jersey, in 1981. Throughout the late 1980s Richard Nixon was sought after and occasionally interviewed by the news media, and more than ten years after the House Judiciary Committee recommended his impeachment, Nixon continued to advise, albeit unofficially, key figures in American politics and government.

> *I let the American people down. And I have to carry that burden with me for the rest of my life.*
> —RICHARD NIXON
> 1977

Further Reading

Anson, Robert S. *Exile: The Unquiet Oblivion of Richard M. Nixon.* New York: Simon & Schuster, 1984.

Brodie, Fawn M. *Richard Nixon: The Shaping of His Character.* New York: Norton, 1981.

Israel, Fred L. *Henry Kissinger.* New York: Chelsea House, 1986.

Nixon, Richard M. *RN: The Memoirs of Richard Nixon.* New York: Grosset & Dunlap, 1977.

———. *Six Crises.* New York: Doubleday, 1962.

White, Theodore H. *The Making of the President 1960.* New York: Atheneum, 1980.

Wills, Garry. *Nixon Agonistes: The Crisis of the Self-Made Man.* New York: Mentor Books, 1979.

Witcover, Jules. *The Resurrection of Richard Nixon.* New York: Putnam, 1970.

Woodward, Bob, and Carl Bernstein. *All The President's Men.* New York: Simon & Schuster, 1974.

Chronology

Jan. 9, 1913	Born Richard Milhous Nixon at Yorba Linda, California
1930	Enters Whittier College
1937	Graduates from Duke University Law School
1941–45	World War II
1942	Works in Washington at the Office of Price Administration
1942–45	Serves in the U.S. Navy as a supply officer
1946	Wins seat in the U.S. House of Representatives
1947–48	Plays a key role in the Alger Hiss case
1950	Elected to the U.S. Senate
1952	Delivers Checkers speech on nationwide television and radio
	Elected vice-president of the United States
1956	Reelected vice-president
1958	Tours Latin America; attacked by mobs in Caracas, Venezuela
1959	Visits Soviet Union; "kitchen debate" with Soviet Premier Khrushchev
1960	Nominated Republican candidate for president; loses election to John F. Kennedy
1962	Publishes *Six Crises*
	Loses race for governorship of California
1963	Joins New York law firm
1964–66	Campaigns nationwide for Republican candidates
1968	Elected president of the United States
1970–71	Orders secret bombings of Cambodia and Laos
July 1971	Pentagon Papers published
June 17, 1972	Break-in at the headquarters of the Democratic National Committee, in the Watergate building in Washington, D.C.
1972–74	Nixon involved in cover-up conspiracy
1972	Becomes first U.S. president to visit China, setting the stage for normalized relations between the two nations
	Visits Soviet Union
Nov. 1972	Reelected president
Jan. 1973	Cease-fire agreement ends direct American involvement in Vietnam
July 1974	Supreme Court rules that the White House tapes must be released; House Judiciary Committee recommends impeachment
Aug. 9, 1974	Nixon resigns from office
1978	Publishes *RN: The Memoirs of Richard Nixon*

Index

Agnew, Spiro, 67, 73, 78, 79, 100, 104
Atlanta, 51
Beijing, 73
Bernstein, Carl, 97
Brezhnev, Leonid, 87, 88
Brown, Pat, 53
Burger, Warren, 92
California, 18, 19, 21, 22, 26, 33, 52, 53, 55, 70, 107
Calley, William, 81
Cambodia, 79, 80, 81, 82, 104
Caracas, 46, 47, 48
Carter, Jimmy, 107
Central Intelligence Agency (CIA), 96
Chambers, Whittaker, 30, 31, 32
"Checkers speech," 39, 40
Chicago, 49, 66
China, 18, 73, 85, 86, 87, 88, 89, 107
Cold war, 27, 28, 32, 33
Colson, Charles, 100
Committee to Reelect the President (CREEP), 14, 98
Congress, U.S., 16, 17, 23, 30, 34, 43, 57, 91, 93
    see also House of Representatives, U.S.; Senate, U.S.
Constitution, U.S., 16, 91, 107
Cronin, John, 29
"Crusade for Political Purity," 37
Dallas, 56
Dean, John, 96, 97, 98, 99, 101
Democratic National Committee, 14, 95, 96
Democratic National Convention (Chicago 1968), 66, 67
Democratic party, 13, 40, 43, 44, 49, 57, 58, 63, 64, 71, 73, 95
Department of Defense, U.S., 82
Department of Justice, U.S., 15
Department of State, U.S., 30, 75
Detroit, 62
Douglas, Helen Gahagan, 33, 34, 42, 67, 103
Duke University, 20, 55
Eagleton, Thomas, 71
Egypt, 95
Ehrlichman, John, 96, 98, 100

Eisenhower, Dwight D., 25, 35, 37, 38, 40, 42, 43, 44, 45, 47, 48, 50, 75
Ellsberg, Daniel, 82, 99
Ervin, Sam, 98
Federal Bureau of Investigation (FBI), 22, 96, 99
Foggy Bottom, 75
Ford, Gerald R., 107
Frost, David, 107
Germany, 23, 76
Goldwater, Bary, 55, 57, 58, 59, 60, 69
Great Depression, 25, 28
Great Society, 56, 57, 58, 60, 63, 69, 91, 94
Great Wall of China, 86
Green Island, 23
Haiphong, 83
Haldeman, H. R., 96, 98, 100
Hanoi, 83, 84
Harvard University, 76
Hiss, Alger, 30, 31, 32, 40, 97
Ho Chi Minh trail, 79
Holmes, Oliver Wendell, 30
House Committee on Un-American Activities (HUAC), 29, 30, 32, 97
House of Representatives, U.S., 15, 16, 25, 26, 29, 35, 73, 101, 107
Houston, 50
Hue, 65
Humphrey, Hubert H., 66, 67, 68, 69
Hunt, E. Howard, 96
Illinois, 52
Internal Revenue Service, U.S., 99, 100
Israel, 95
Jackson State College, 81
Japan, 23, 25, 85
Job Corps, 94
Johnson, Lyndon B., 49, 56, 57, 58, 60, 61, 63, 64, 65, 66, 67, 68, 69, 70, 71, 82, 83, 94, 99
Kennedy, John F., 49, 50, 51, 52, 55, 56, 69, 82, 99
Kennedy, Robert, 64, 66, 67, 69
Kent State University, 81
Kersten, Charles, 29
Khe Sanh, 65
Khmer Rouge, 79, 80

Khrushchev, Nikita, 48, 49
King, Martin Luther, Jr., 51, 52, 62, 66
Kissinger, Henry, 76, 83, 84, 85, 86, 87, 88, 89
"kitchen debate," 49
Korea, 33, 40, 41
Ku Klux Klan, 51
Labor Committee, 29
Laos, 79, 80, 81, 82
Le Duc Tho, 83
Leaders, 107
Liddy, G. Gordon, 96
Life, 49
Lodge, Henry Cabot, 49
Lon Nol, 79, 80
Los Angeles, 20
Los Angeles Times, 34
Mao Zedong, 86
McCarthy, Eugene, 64, 67
McCarthy, Joseph, 41, 42, 43
McCord, James, 98
McGovern, George, 13, 14, 71
Miami, 67, 73
Mitchell, John, 95, 96, 100
Moscow, 46, 48, 73, 88
Muskie, Edmund S., 67
My Lai massacre, 81, 82
National Catholic Welfare Conference, 29
National Institutes of Health, 94
National Security Council, 76
New Deal, 26
New Federalism, 91
New Hampshire, 64, 65
New York City, 32, 55, 104, 107
New York Times, The, 82
Newark, 62
Nixon, Arthur (brother), 19
Nixon, Frank (father), 19
Nixon, Hannah (mother), 19
Nixon, Harold (brother), 19
Nixon, Julie (daughter), 52, 55
Nixon, Pat Ryan (wife), 22, 39, 52
Nixon, Richard Milhous
    anticommunist, 25, 27, 29, 31, 33, 34, 40, 41, 40, 42, 43, 49, 103
    birth, 19

congressman, 25, 29, 30, 31, 33
early years, 19, 20, 21
education, 20
evaluation of presidency, 103–107
foreign policy and, 75, 76, 79, 80, 81, 85–89
Hiss case and, 31, 32, 33
lawyer, 22
marriage, 22
pardoned, 107
president, 68, 69, 72, 73, 91, 92, 93, 94, 95, 99, 104
presidential election of 1960 and, 49–52
resignation, 13, 18, 101
senator, 25, 35
vice-president, 25, 41, 42, 43, 44, 45, 46, 48, 49, 75
Vietnam War and, 77, 78, 79, 80, 84, 85, 89
Watergate and, 15–18, 95–98, 100, 101, 104
Nixon, Tricia (daughter), 39, 52, 55
Nixon Doctrine, 86
North Vietnam, 60, 61, 65, 77, 83, 84, 85, 89
Office of Economic Opportunity (OEO), 94
Office of Price Administration (OPA), 23
Organization of Petroleum Exporting Countries (OPEC), 95
Paris peace talks, 68, 83
Peiking *see* Beijing
Pentagon Papers, 82, 99
"Pumpkin Papers," 31
Real Peace, 107
Real War, The, 107
Rebozo, Bebe, 100
Republican party, 13, 27, 33, 35, 37, 41, 42, 43, 44, 55, 57, 59, 60, 103
RN: The Memoirs of Richard Nixon, 107
Rogers, William, 75
Roosevelt, Franklin D., 26, 28
Sadat, Anwar, 107
Saddle River, 107
Saigon, 65
SALT I (Strategic Arms Limitation Talks), 88
San Clemente, 107

Secret Service, U.S.,   46, 47
Senate, U.S.,   16, 25, 33, 35, 42, 73, 92, 98,
     100, 101
Sirica, John, 97, 98
Six Crises, 52
South Vietnam,   60, 77, 78, 79, 80, 82, 83,
     84, 85, 89
Soviet Union,   18, 27, 28, 29, 48, 73, 85, 86,
     88, 89
Spain,   29
Sparkman, John,   39
Stalin, Joseph,   28
Stevenson, Adlai,   39, 40, 44
Supreme Court, U.S.,   82, 92, 101
Syria,   95
Tet offensive,   65
Texas,   52
Time,   30
Truman, Harry S.,   30
United Nations,   30, 86, 89
University of California, San Diego,   22

Viet Cong,   60, 65, 79
Vietnam War,   18, 55, 60, 61, 62, 63, 65, 67,
     68, 70, 76, 77, 78, 79, 82, 84, 87, 88,
     89, 94, 95
"Vietnamization,"   78, 79, 80
Voorhis, Jerry,   26, 27, 29, 33, 42, 67, 103
Yom Kippur War,   95, 107
Yorba Linda,   19
Warren, Earl,   92
Washington, D.C.,   14, 19, 23, 33, 47, 62,
     64–70, 81, 91
Washington Post, The,   97
Watergate affair,   14–17, 95–98, 100, 105
White House,   13, 14, 18, 42, 72, 73, 75, 93,
     96, 97, 98, 99, 104
"White House Plumbers,"   82, 99
Whittier,   19, 22, 23
Whittier College,   20, 22
World War II,   23, 25, 29, 35, 77, 85, 86,
     89
Woodward, Bob,   97

C. Peter Ripley was educated at Florida State University and taught in a federal prison and at Yale before returning to Florida State, where he now teaches history. He has written several books and scholarly articles, many of them on Afro-American history. He teaches a course on America in the 1960s and is the author of ROBERT KENNEDY in the Chelsea House series WORLD LEADERS—PAST & PRESENT.

Arthur M. Schlesinger, jr., taught history at Harvard for many years and is currently Albert Schweitzer Professor of the Humanities at City University of New York. He is the author of numerous highly praised works in American history and has twice been awarded the Pulitzer Prize. He served in the White House as special assistant to Presidents Kennedy and Johnson.